BLOOD BROOK

A Naturalist's Home Ground

Ted Levin

CHELSEA GREEN PUBLISHING COMPANY
Post Mills, Vermont

Portions of this book have appeared in or been adapted from chapters in *The Curious Naturalist*, published by the National Geographic Society, 1991. Quotation from *Book of Days* by Hal Borland is reprinted by permission of Random House, Inc., copyright 1976 by Alfred A. Knopf, Inc., New York. Quotation from *The Spider* by John Compton is reprinted by permission of Nick Lyons Books, copyright 1987 by Nick Lyons Books, New York.

1   2   3   4   5   6   7   8   9   10

Library of Congress Cataloging-in-Publication Data

Levin, Ted
Blood Brook: a naturalist's home ground / Ted Levin
p. cm.
ISBN 0-930031-56-3 (cloth: alk. paper): $21.95
ISBN 0-930031-60-1 (paper): $14.95
1. Natural history. 2. Natural history—New England. I. Title.
QH81.L65 1992   92-16626
508.743'6—dc20   CIP

For Joan and John

Contents

Prologue

Blood Brook is a humble stream. For three miles its waters cut through a single narrow valley in east-central Vermont, draining less than three and a half square miles of woods and meadows before emptying into a cattail marsh on the north end of Lake Fairlee. We live high in the valley, on a hill a hundred yards above the rushing water. From my front yard I see Blood Brook blinking in the sun as it coils through ranks of goldenrod and reeds, flanked by a dark wall of pine and the somber trunks of November maple. The brook and its attendant valley quicken my curiosity far out of proportion to its size. This is my home.

I live with my wife, Linny, a naturalist, and our son Casey, who is five. Our passive solar house faces the path of the sun. Bermed into a hill, the north side of the house is windowless and sheltered from winter wind. Thick thermal glass extends from the roofline almost to the floor on the south side. When I'm inside, I look at the world as though from a fish bowl, straight down the valley, over a mosaic of meadows and woods, the roofs of old farmhouses and a barn, across stone-cold maples and oaks to Potato Hill and High Peak, southeast beyond Lake Fairlee. I cannot see the lake, but on cold autumn mornings its breath hangs below High Peak or creeps up the valley, and Blood Brook metamorphoses into primal America.

When a low October cloud ceiling forces migrating yellow-rumped warblers closer to the ground, the window halts them. Reading in bed, I hear tiny, fragile skulls striking glass. Chick-adees and evening grosbeaks hit the window, too, yet their colli-sions are seldom fatal because these birds, darting to and from our bird-feeding station, don't have enough momentum when they strike to cause serious damage. Instead, feeder birds bounce off the window, then regain control of their flight, leaving a tiny yellow or gray feather to mark the spot.

East of our house, Blood Brook curls around a spring-fed pond, which the previous landowner dug ten years ago. In early spring wood ducks, mallards, and black ducks idle on the pond. When wood frog tadpoles mature in early summer, hungry king-fishers cackle from the pondside's dead elm. In late summer a great blue heron stalks frogs and tadpoles from the shoreline, and an American bittern stands in the cattail patch on the pond's north end, waiting. In September, yellowlegs stop by. I am sur-prised. To a wayfaring sandpiper, cruising several thousand feet above the valley, the pond must appear as no more than a drop of water, rimmed by mud. Wouldn't Lake Fairlee or the Connecticut River, with its parallel banks running uninterrupted south to Long Island Sound, look more inviting, promise more food? I fol-low the yellowlegs, slim, gray and white, with binoculars. They teeter around the pond—rump up, rump down—picking at mud-dwelling invertebrates. Through the cattails. Around a boulder. Past a withered cardinal flower. Their circuit complete, they head out for another hemisphere.

Runoff from the pond spills through a pipe into the brook, which then wends its way down the valley to the lake. East of the brook a belt of woods reaches uphill to the edge of Bloodbrook

Road. Beyond the road the land rises abruptly to Bald Top, which from where I sit appears as a long, high ridge. Up there the forest is big, extending northeast toward Bradford. Black bears visit for September blackberries; ravens and red-tailed hawks float above Bald Top, circling, circling, circling, plying invisible currents deflected upward from the valley.

The terrain rises gently to the west, dips, rises, dips, and rises again, before dropping steeply into the longer, wider, more fertile valley of Middle Brook, which pours into Lake Fairlee about a mile southwest of the Blood Brook marshes. When bears finish Bald Top's berries, they cross Blood Brook, dig quiescent yellow jackets or bat down sweet corn from my neighbor's garden, and then follow the setting sun to Middle Brook, to gorge on wild apples. The western slope of the valley supports pine, maple, red oak, and beech, smaller trees than those that grow on Bald Top. Running uphill, a stone wall passes our house, follows the tree line for a quarter mile, turns into the woods, and emerges on the edge of Bloodbrook Road. Chipmunks and shrews and milk snakes live among the stones.

A gnarled, fifty-foot-tall maple with a trifurcated trunk, low, lateral branches, and a broad, broken crown grows southeast of the house. As in a well-composed photograph, the tree provides a point of focus in the meadowed foreground, directing my eye eastward toward the pond. I catch a glimpse of Blood Brook and the middle-distant woods, then my gaze travels up Bald Top and High Peak. Without the maple, my view of the valley would lack scale and the birds would lack a way station, for the tree affords the only perch between Blood Brook and the gentle western slope of the valley, more than two hundred yards of perennial grasses and wildflowers. Downy and hairy woodpeckers forage insects from its pleated trunk. White-breasted nuthatches hide sunflower seeds in the crotches of twigs. Purple finches, wine-red and quick to sing, prune buds, then wipe their bills along a branch, leaving a residue of tiny brown bud scales.

I want to consort with my home ground, to know the language of the brook, the hill, the valley, and the lake; to hear trees crack on cold, black January nights and feel the wind pulling ravens upward to Bald Top. I want to know how the seasons and years play upon or against the land, and see how tendrils connect observer and observed across space and time, to distant lands and epochs. I seek a life on this land the way a boy seeks baseball, its untimed, impartial rhythms, its idle moments, its sudden drama. Through it all, I wait for the delicious delusion that I actually know what's going on.

In early spring I roam the Southwest for four weeks. Returning home after these long excursions is not easy, for the valley is still cold and wet and gray, almost as dreary as when I left. I walk through the woods: sugar maple buds are small; spotted salamanders have not yet spawned; and, except for the arrival of phoebes and the flowering of coltsfoot, there are few visible suggestions of spring.

I look at Bald Top, and all I see are trees, trees, trees, rooted in thick, rich, stony soil which masks the bare bones of the land. After a month in the desert, the view here seems too close, too tight, too confining. I cannot follow the sun the length of its arc across the Vermont sky; sunrises and sunsets are hidden by rows of ancient, fertile hills on either side. Where are the pastel clouds, lavender and pink, leading edges etched with green and violet, that start at the desert horizon, just above the setting sun, and extend to the zenith? Where are the rainbow sundogs? Where is the prairie falcon in California's Borrego Badlands sweeping below me through a thousand-foot-deep gorge lined with parallel ridges of eroded sandstone, the color of which changes with the angle of the sun?

Compelled to travel and often depressed when I return to find winter still lingering, I must let the rivulets of my life, which seem to flow asunder, run together like the water of this valley. I seek a fresh perspective, another view, to see the whole of North America embodied in Blood Brook.

I grew up in a conservative Jewish home on the south shore of Long Island. My father's father was a successful businessman who manufactured and sold men's clothing. He employed many family members, including my father, and traveled a good deal, averaging five months on the road each year. During the summer of 1948 he was stricken by a malignant brain tumor and was found by a chambermaid lying in a coma on the floor of a California hotel room, three thousand miles from home.

My mother's father, an orthodox Jewish scholar, went from Ellis Island directly to Toledo, Ohio. New York City was not his bowl of borscht. He fasted whenever he read the Torah, which was more than once a week, taught Hebrew at the local synagogue, and made very little money, but he was apparently very happy; he died of lip cancer from smoking too many cigars.

Both grandfathers fled anti-Semitism in czarist Russia and emigrated to the United States around 1900. As far as I know, neither one read John Muir, although my mother's family did grow their own vegetables and raise and slaughter their own beef. Both grandfathers died before I was born.

Beyond love for my family, I had faith in three things when I was ten years old: the New York Yankees; a benevolent God who had a special place in his omnipresent heart for Jews; and nature, which was in the full, rounded sense predictable. Tropical storms came in autumn, snow in winter, and frogs in spring. In summer the Atlantic was warm and swimmable.

My faith in the first two has since crumbled. When I was twelve, I began to question God's kind and just aspects. Why, I asked my Hebrew teacher, was I consigned to a life without grand-fathers? The Lord works in mysterious ways, I was told. Why, then, did he permit six million Jews to die in Nazi Europe? Because of the Holocaust, my teacher said, Jews came home to Israel: in effect this was the price for the Promised Land. But is any pact worth six million lives and eternal damnation?

After carefully weighing my teacher's line of reasoning I realized that God, if he existed at all, played no favorites. He was completely impartial, like a volcano or an earthquake or a hurricane.

By the time I was sixteen, the Yankees had fallen from glory and become a mediocre baseball team. Mickey Mantle, his legs torn to pieces, could no longer hit and run, and his astonishing career collapsed before my eyes.

Only my love of nature survived adolescence. Now, I gauge my life by the swing of the seasons. Nature is impartial and omnipresent, an integrated community of lesser and greater beings who are slowly transforming the whole as the whole slowly transforms them, one organism, one community of organisms changing into another. I've learned that relationships between living things are as important as the animals and plants themselves. How can we know the season from the bird?

Nature is beautiful and dangerous, boring and inspirational, providing story after story from the recesses of the past and into the unimagined future, endless information presented in an infinite number of ways. Nature is self-nourishing, self-healing, self-cleansing, self-regulating. Defiled or defaced, she rebounds with icy cold indifference. Still awed, I face the seasons.

Like Abraham, who made a covenant with God, I must make a covenant with the land—an unbridled agreement to couple with the forces of life and let them move through me, now and forever. Such a covenant begins at home in my own backyard.

Casey engages the valley effortlessly, unconsciously. He grows lemon sorrel and cherry tomatoes, picks blueberries and raspberries, and shakes wild apples from low branches, collecting the bounty for cider. He catches garter snakes and helps me measure and sex them. I clip a section of one of their belly scales to mark them; Casey then gives the snakes a meal of earthworms, which he gathers from the roots of garden plants, and releases them. He nets frogs and newts, watches butterflies emerge and tadpoles transform, and relocates red efts to his secret places.

Rose-breasted grosbeaks draw his burgeoning imagination beyond the valley, beyond even our watershed. Each winter he asks after these birds, then claps in joy when they return in spring. He calls them simply "rosey"—as in dad rosey, mom rosey, two roseys—and finds them without me, by sight and sound. He recognizes our three resident dads by the red of their bibs. The grosbeak's distinctive call note, an emphatic peek, and its robinesque song cascade from the maple while Casey weeds his lemon sorrel. And he watches raptly as fledglings—whose feathers and muscles and bones, he knows, are transformed sunflower seeds—come to the feeder in July, wings quivering, mouths open, begging to be fed.

One afternoon a rosey flew to the feeder, still singing, and red underwings flashed like a semaphore. A hummingbird hovered in front of the grosbeak, scrutinizing his red breast. Satisfied that there were no rewards beyond the color, the hummingbird flew to the feeder. Casey laughed.

He is beginning to sense what John Hay calls "earth's immortal consistencies." He knows that the planet circles the sun once each year and that his birthday arrives when wild strawberries ripen, when turtles leave the lake to lay their eggs, and when the rosey carols.

The study of nature begins at home, with a knowledge of

local geography and an attempt to be part of the ebb and flow of one's backyard, the only place where you'll be more than a visitor. Native people had this intimacy. I sense it in Western Abenaki myths and legends, which spring from the hills; vivid and home-grown, these tales are as necessary as science to bring the land to life. Where else but in Indian stories do bears become gods; beams of sunlight, flowers? Where else do seasons resolve into beings?

How do I begin to learn about my land, about the nuances of local geography, about the creases and folds of the Connecticut Valley, those subtle characteristics that make Bald Top different from Potato Hill, and the morning light different from that of the evening? I go outside. Stay outside. I ask questions of the people who make their living by reading the land—the forester, the farmer. I go to the library and read stories from the land: scientific journals, poems, and fiction. I dream.

Last night I dreamed of a big silver-tipped grizzly bear. A lunatic, two-story-tall bear that ran through the shoals of a salmon stream, upright, his long-clawed front paws madly waving like a man hailing a cab. This was not an incurable romantic's animal dream, in which a conversational bear chatted about issues great and small. Perched on a crumbling, wafer-thin ledge, with my back pressed against rock and my toes curled inward I wobbled, clutching stones, helpless and afraid in the path of an irascible behemoth. This was a serious dream, for I had two strikes against me, with two outs, in the bottom of the ninth. Fortunately, I woke up.

I always wake up when death stalks my dreams. Although the bear never makes a kill, he keeps me alert and heightens my senses. When I lived by the ocean, a shark out of a Peter Benchley movie with a Cuisinart mouth was my occasional dream-time antagonist. The shark didn't keep me out of the water and the grizzly won't keep me from the rocky West. In fact, both dream animals amplify my interest in nature by reminding me that people don't always dominate the food pyramid.

Knowing that bears as big as Buicks are out there, in some remote and crinkled recess of the continent, reassures me. Although I cannot see them in Vermont, I can dream of them. And when I finally see a wild grizzly, I'm sure the size and power and potential threat the bear poses to me will take away my breath, in a way no waterfall or colored hillside could ever do.

Predator and prey are bound in an intricate, evolutionary relationship. The behavior of white-tailed deer—their resoluteness, gracefulness, and swiftness—was honed by their proximity to wolves and mountain lions. Without the primal stimulation of predators, deer aren't truly wild; they aren't deer. Yet now, cushioned by a lack of hazards in an increasingly developed environment, deer have had their fitness compromised and are evolving toward complacency, slowly softened by an easier life.

Do Blood Brook's deer still dream of the wolf? Or honeybees of the ambush bug? Do suckers dream of the otter? Do hare dream of the bobcat? I doubt that domestic sheep dream of coyotes. These vapid lawn ornaments are merely sacrificial lambs when faced with a hungry, intelligent predator. Some don't even bleat as their companions are being eaten. We've bred sheep to be this way, of course: woolly, meaty, and stupid, virtually cut off from the rhythms of their pastures.

Are we any different than sheep? Thoroughly domesticated and totally dependent on the consumption of less-than-essential commodities, some of which come from regions of the Earth we'll never see, we squander irreplaceable natural resources. Our slash-and-burn lifestyles are driving us into an impoverished future.

Leopards and lions no doubt whetted the senses of Pliocene humans, shaping both their dreams and their lives. Pleistocene cave bears performed the same service for the earliest Eurasians, and in the North American West the silver-tipped grizzly stalked both the valleys and the sleeping minds of Native Americans.

My senses are dull, duller than I'd like. Although I can hear the Blackburnian warbler's falsetto high in a spruce, I cannot feel the gaze of the bobcat or smell the presence of a moose. The dream bear reminded me of what's missing from my life, of how a subtle, irreplaceable edge to my being has been filed down.

I hope to sharpen that edge, to see how one small valley, as a microcosm, entwines with the rest of the biosphere and to see if finding my valley will mean finding myself.

As I head for breakfast, a male northern oriole, orange as the rising sun and full of verve, hops on the windowsill. Engaged in illusionary warfare, the bird rails against his own image. Every four or five seconds he jumps into the air with half-cocked wings, feet extended perpendicular to his body, and taps the window with his bill, then sings, a series of loud, clear, flutey notes, sweet as the May morning. Still cool from the night, the window holds the bird's breath for a moment: oriole fog, no bigger than a nickel, condensing, then evaporating.

Descending
Blood Brook

Before me lies a handsome topographical map from the United States Geological Survey, labeled "Fairlee Quadrangle 1981." Blood Brook is a crooked, sporadic blue line that runs south from the 1400-foot contour on Spaulding Hill to the lake. Two hills are noted on either side, Bald Top on the east and an unnamed ridge on the west. On the eastern side, the map's brown contour lines are crowded closely together. Here, on steeper land, four intermittent streams feed the brook, each one a fractured blue line. Three others enter from the west, along with a permanent stream that joins Blood Brook an eighth of a mile upstream from Lake Fairlee.

On the map, half a mile down Spaulding Hill on the 1100-foot contour, Blood Brook finally gains some measure of credibility with the cartographer, who connects the dots to declare it a year-round brook. Over its brief, three-mile-long course, the brook descends 721 feet, a drop that guarantees riffles and little falls.

1

At Lake Fairlee's outlet, an unnamed fork of the East Branch
of the Ompompanoosuc River begins an eight-mile run toward
the West Branch. The East and West Branches join the Connecticut, New England's largest river, at Pompanoosuc, in the township
of Norwich. I recently drove south to Old Lyme, Connecticut, to
see the big river filter through a maze of fertile salt marshes as it
enters Long Island Sound, the end of my extended watershed,
two hundred miles from the sources. Like a salmon or a shad
seeking its natal current, I put my finger into the water at the
river's mouth and tasted. I wish I could report that there was a
deep stirring inside me, a cellular or hormonal recognition, transporting me to a little brook and a narrow valley tucked in the
folded countryside of east-central Vermont, but nothing much
happened.

Now, in October, walking upstream along the flank of
Spaulding Hill, I search for Blood Brook's headwaters. To my sur-
prise, I find not one source but many sources scattered over the
south side of the hill, mere puddles in the spongy soil. These
seeps, as hydrologists call them, are sites where groundwater,
forced up by an impenetrable layer of rock, trickles to the surface.
A spring is formed in the same way but has a greater flow. The
water in my muddy puddles, forced upward by some invisible geologic configuration, "began" as rain or snowmelt, perhaps years
ago. Absorbed by porous soil, rain has threaded its way through
fissures in the rock to emerge at my feet on Spaulding Hill. I am
reminded of this each winter as I drive along the interstate, admiring the enormous ice formations that decorate the sheer granite walls where the highway department's blasting has broken into
underground streams.

There are so many headstreams to Blood Brook, so many av-
enues to walk, that my primitive field sketch begins to look more
like a network of capillaries than a brook. Although seeps stay

free of snow cover longer than the surrounding land and are primary winter foraging sites for raccoons, skunks, and particularly for wild turkeys, which I've since watched scratching through the thin snow crust to find seeds and nuts, they entertain only mosquitoes now. Eventually, I give up searching and drawing, and settle on a more pragmatic task: following the flow downstream through my valley.

Down the hill in our yard, where the brook becomes a real brook, I step into my waders, adjust the straps, and head up across my neighbor's meadow, a quarter mile above our house, where alders and willows crowd the brook, woodcocks gather in April, yellowthroats in May, and a patch of wetland wildflowers— marsh marigold, jewelweed, joe-pye weed—attracts bees, wasps, and ruby-throated hummingbirds in summer. In the pines near the meadow, the brook funnels through a notch on a slippery, water-polished ledge, then drops over the edge in a wavering curtain over the edge to a pool below. I can hear the gurgle from my front yard. A pool above the ledge contains three sculpins. They see my shadow and dart for safety into a ball of roots in the shade of an undercut bank. I probe around with a stick. Two high-strung little fish, no more than two inches long and propelled by winglike pectoral fins, scoot across the bottom, leaving an expanding line of sediment in their wake.

A sculpin looks as if someone had stepped on its head, flattening its forehead and forcing the eyes to pop up like a frog's. In fact, a sculpin looks like a composite, a fish put together of spare parts: mouth of a bass, head of a flatfish, body of a trout, a frog's eyes and seal flippers for fins. I keep probing. Sculpins continue to flee, and six plumes of silt spread out and merge into a thick, brown screen. The pool is so stirred up that I can no longer follow the fish.

Another gathering of sculpins assembles in some riffles fifty

3

yards upstream. Not wishing to disturb them, I watch from the bank. Each sculpin faces into the current, tight to the pebbles, its head flat on the bottom, its large pectoral fins pressed against the stones. Together with tiny pelvic fins that are set close together and far forward on the body, the thick pectorals form a friction plate that keeps the sculpin from being swept downstream. Slowly the little fish forage along the bottom for aquatic insects. Sculpins have large mouths for their size, big enough to engulf stonefly and mayfly nymphs. Sculpins scan the water with what seems to me an almost mechanical beat, their eyes swiveling back and forth, up and down, like a pair of periscopes mounted on ball-and-socket joints. I lean out and my shadow stretches across the brook. Sculpins sense my presence and scatter.

Returning downstream, I stroll through Blood Brook past our pond. A dozen water striders skate across a pool, in and out of my reflection. With long, hair-thin legs, these insects glide, hop, and stand on the water, supported by surface tension, the tight, stretchy film of water molecules which occurs at the inter-face of air and water. Water striders use the upper side of the sur-face film for support; other creatures use its lower side. I've seen a hydra, its tentacles dangling into the water below, and rafts of mosquito eggs and larvae suspended upside-down from the sur-face tension. Once I saw a little snail creeping along on the under surface of a glass-smooth pond as though along an aquarium wall.

The strider's long legs distribute its weight, and tiny, waxy hairs repel water so that the insect's feet dimple the surface with-out breaking through. Whenever I cross a sandy stream bed, I pause with my head hanging over the bank, caught in the spell of the striders' shadows, balloonlike shapes cast on the light-colored bottom. Formed where a leg depresses the surface, these shadows twitch and jerk as the strider glides by, illustrating the subtle in-terplay of insect and water and air.

The dark and rocky bottom of Blood Brook camouflages the

water striders' shadows. A long, middle pair of legs rows the insect forward while the hind pair trails and the short front pair rests on the surface, ready to grab food. Through sensory organs in their legs, striders receive surface tension vibrations. These are generally used to orient the striders to their prey, but in spring, each male vibrates the surface with his middle legs, sending a rippling species-specific love note to females.

I drop a mosquito on the water. A strider skates over. Holding the mosquito with its forelegs, the strider drills and drains it with its styletlike mouth and then discards it. A mosquito husk drifts downstream.

During the summer, a colony of black-winged damselflies patrols this section of Blood Brook, flying above the striders through leaf-filtered light or perching on overhanging witch hazel branches with their black wings spread and their metallic green abdomens raised. Now, damselfly nymphs crawl below the striders, and last summer's adults mulch the banks of the brook.

I leave the pool and pass through a neighboring pasture, following a cow path downhill onto a broad grassy plain. A stream enters the pasture from the east, drips from a culvert and is ground into a long, muddy swath by cattle. Two unmapped tributaries, both heavily trampled, enter from the west, adding to the widening belt of mud. Blood Brook itself flows deep and swift through a channel in the pasture, gathering force and volume for its descent.

The cattle spot me and move toward me. Their pace quickens; mine, too. I'm running now, my hands pinned to my shoulders, grasping my wader straps, binoculars banging against my chest. I glance over my shoulder. This is not a pastoral scene of the Vermont Holstein T-shirt ilk—these are squat Herefords, bovine vigilantes, and they're charging. I win the race to the gate and, half vaulting, half kicking, scramble over the top.

Under the hemlocks, Blood Brook takes on a wildness, tumbling down terraced ledges, rushing around boulders, fretting over rocks. In the tree-cooled waters, I see brook trout fingerlings, no more than a few inches long. During the summer they gathered in grottos beneath the overhanging bank and patrolled nearby pools for terrestrial insects trapped by the surface film or mayflies just leaving the water. Where the brook rushes over stones, they checked for larvae of algae-feeding caddisflies, for nymphs of mayflies and stoneflies, for damselflies, and maybe even sculpin fry. Now suspended in the current, hungry trout wait for what little October has to offer them. Spotting me, they're gone, passing through my field of vision so quickly that I'm not sure I've seen a fish or a speck of sunlight.

Sneaking up on a brook trout is an acquired skill. Lying motionless on the bank, I see the trout's distinctive white stripe on the leading edge of the lower fins, dark squiggles cover an olive-green back. If it moves into the light, the large yellow spots that pepper a trout's sides become visible. But when a live brook trout rests in someone's creel, I can see subtler colors: the iridescent aqua-blue sides with small blue-haloed red spots, the orange-tinted fins.

Brook trout are actually char, members of the genus *Salvelinus*, which includes lake trout. Both brook and lake trout descended from a common ancestor in eastern North America during the Pliocene epoch, about two to five million years ago. According to the fossil record, lake trout have changed very little since then, confining themselves to relatively stable, deep-water lakes across the northern half of the continent from coast to coast and above the Arctic Circle. Native brook trout remain an Atlantic drainage fish, yet they have adapted to a much wider range of habitats than their lacustrine cousins: they live in beaver ponds and cold-water lakes, and in streams ranging in size from Blood Brook to the Connecticut River. In Maine and the Canadian Maritimes, an anadromous race of brook trout comes inland to spawn from the sea.

Trout line up in the current behind the half-submerged trunk of an old white pine. One. Two. Three. . . . Eleven. Twelve. They wait for food, paying no attention to me. Water spills over the smooth, bare wood. The fish remain suspended in place, inhaling the current as it pours over them.

I splinter a white pine twig into little pieces and flick them into the brook. A trout rises and is joined by two more. One takes the wood in its mouth, settles in front of the trunk, then realizes it has been tricked. Spit from the trout, my wooden lure bobs to the surface.

Because they live in swift-flowing water, these brook trout must be adept at holding their position in the current or be swept downstream. A streamlined body, tapered at both ends, widest just in front of a dorsal fin that is a little more than a third of the way down its length, makes for perfect ballast in water. The trout undulate their bodies against the flow and fan their broad, square tails, while their fine scales form an almost frictionless surface in the rushing water. Each trout extends its dorsal fin, which billows in the current, stabilizing the fish.

Brook trout capture prey at all levels in the water. Their eyes furnish excellent binocular vision in front and above. Although laterally their eyes are largely monocular, they can scan the bottom too.

If hungry trout come to wood, I muse, they'll love cluster flies. I return home and pick twenty or so from my office window, where a congregation is assembled in the sun, and surgically remove a wing from each so that when the flies hit the water they will spin in a circle, broadcasting concentric distress signals as they float downstream.

The next afternoon, I check my topographical map for the easiest access to the trout, gather up the flies in a baby food jar, and drive toward Lake Fairlee. Parking, I enter the woods, the flies buzzing in my pocket, cross a wet meadow, and intersect Blood Brook below the smooth white pine. A hundred yards downstream stands a pine. Its scoured roots bend around a cavern in the undercut bank, keeping out all but the most skillfully cast flies. A seven-inch male whose belly and sides are washed in red and whose lower jaw is a slightly enlarged tends a five-inch female. They see me and swim downstream.

My feet hooked under pine roots, my right hand wedged against a yellow birch, I peer over the lip of the bank. Fourteen trout that range in size from two to four inches gather, two and three abreast. I shake out the cluster flies. A trout rises. Hits. Another rises. Hits. And another. Eventually, there are two flies, then one. As I stare at the remaining fly, a trout shoots up from the grotto.

I walk a hundred yards downstream. A patch of riffles that in early May had entertained innumerable spawning white suckers now is quiet by comparison. I turn over a stone: a dusky salamander launches into the current and quickly disappears from view. A second stone yields two mayfly nymphs. Unlike the salamander, they are not in a hurry and creep over an adjacent stone.

In spring these shoals seethe with foot-long suckers, fins thrashing at the surface, so many fish that I can catch them with my hands. Females lay thousands of eggs, as males, held in place by the friction of rough tubercles along the sides of their bodies, press against them, competing to spray milk-colored milt over the eggs. One female discharged a fusillade of yellowish orange eggs as I held her. Sucker eggs stick to everything—rocks, roots, my waders. Three weeks later, after the adults return from the brook to vacuum food off the bottom of Lake Fairlee, sucker fry hatch in the shoals.

Spawning suckers provoke migrating osprey, raccoons, mink,

and red fox. The piles of otter scat along the high bank of both Blood and Middle brooks suggest that local otter feed on little else. And when sucker eggs hatch, kingfishers arrive, and begin busily feeding their own young. By October, Earth has traveled halfway around the sun, the water is shallower, and the fry are long gone. Now, otter roam the lake and kingfishers fly south.

Beyond the riffle, the brook widens and slows. A gray sandbar reaches into quiet water. Deer drink here and leave deep, cloven prints, sunk to the dewclaws. One deer trail crosses an unnamed hill, another the meadow. I can tell from the tracks that a raccoon has traversed the west bank, walked out on the bar, reached into the brook with his sensitive forepaws, and then moved on. A pileated woodpecker laughs in the distance.

A recent article in the *New York Times* challenges the old notion of a brook as a single flowing body of water with a main channel. Ecologists now believe there is a subterranean world, a brook beneath a brook, a river beneath a river, where a separate stream of groundwater spreads out and flows below the visible brook, interacting with it, and nourishing it. A maze of underground channels carries water and supports aquatic insects, worms, crustacea, and nitrogen-fixing bacteria, all of which contribute to the health of Blood Brook. I cannot see the watery current below my feet, or the busy movements of aquatic troglodytes, but I imagine that the subterranean denizens, like the creatures of the visible brook, slow down and shift activity to the beat of the canting Earth, as winter ineluctably overtakes autumn.

On the Fairlee Quadrangle map, the 427-acre lake looks like a giant tadpole, its tail swung to the north to meet Blood Brook, its head southwest, feeding the unnamed fork of the Ompompanoosuc's East Branch. A half mile wide at its widest point, and with more than six miles of shoreline, Lake Fairlee appears on road maps yet is small enough to be known intimately. Although it is fed by seven streams (three of which dry up by August), Middle Brook and Blood Brook are Lake Fairlee's main life lines, its umbilical connections to the green hills beyond. Choked with acres of cattails and sedges that eventually deepen to zones of floating and then submerged vegetation, the brooks' two marshes form the lake's placenta, where dark clouds of mustachioed bullheads school in the shallows.

I secure my kayak on the car, drive to the lake, and park where Blood Brook unloads its cargo. The land here is flat and sandy, worn by shifting water.

In the kayak I paddle to a muskrat lodge on the edge of the marsh, a three-foot-high stack of cattails and water lilies plastered with mud and decorated with two cigarette packages. The lodge is at the center of a patch of stubby cattails, each stalk neatly cut below the water line. Muskrats have cut the cattails for insulation and carried them back to the lodge with their forepaws. Unlike beaver, muskrats gather food all winter, digging roots, tubers, rhizomes, and the occasional clam below the ice. One morning last winter while lying on black ice, I watched a muskrat swim below me. He held a tuber in his forepaws. His fur shed streaks of shiny, silver bubbles that rose and stuck against the under surface of the ice like strings of pearls. Following, I slid on my belly along the ice until the muskrat dove from sight.

In summer this corner of the marsh sponsors coteries of white-winged skimmers, one of the most common species of dragonflies around Lake Fairlee, which patrol for mosquitoes, chase one another, and mate in midflight. Sitting in my kayak last summer, I collected dozens of the skimmers' inch-long nymphal exoskeletons, bright and shiny, like polished brass medallions, from the stems of bullhead lilies. I see none today.

Male dragonflies set up territories above the marsh, dividing the shoreline into well-defined segments; then they wait for females to enter their air spaces. Whenever a male violates another's boundaries, the resident drives him away. When a female darts over the marsh, nearby males rush after her. The first male to arrive, usually the owner of the closest territory, clasps her behind the head with his cerci, a pair of appendages which protrude from the end of his abdomen like curved tweezers. While the male holds her neck, the female reaches around with the tip of her abdomen and retrieves a packet of sperm from a storage chamber below his second abdominal segment. The affair lasts but a few seconds, one reaching over and the other reaching under, as the two dragonflies fly in tandem.

When copulation ends, the male, still clasping the female's neck, leads her to an egg-depositing site in his territory, near the water lilies and cattails, close to where I now sit in my kayak. He relaxes his grip, then guards her as she dips to the surface and strikes her abdomen against the water, releasing streams of glistening eggs with each strike. An unattended female may be driven from the water by another male who also clasps her and repeats the entire mating process. In such an event, the sperm of the first male are forced deeper into the female's sperm storage organ. Since sperm closest to the surface of the female's storage organ fertilize the eggs, the efforts of the first male are wasted. A female accepts several mates but uses only the sperm of the last mate for fertilization—a last-in, first-out system. To contribute his genetic material to the next generation, a male must guard his mate.

The marsh overflows with sexual energy in August. White-tailed skimmers mate up to eighty times in an afternoon. Dragonflies are locked in tandem flights. Female dragonflies strike the water with their abdomens. Dragonflies eat mosquitoes and deer flies, and are eaten by birds. Dragonflies ride my kayak. Dragonflies chase dragonflies.

I watch as a female skimmer drops to the water, guarded by a male, and injects her eggs below the surface. She rises: a male red-winged blackbird meets her. Four transparent dragonfly wings, veined like flower petals and translucent in the sunlight, float down to the water as dozens of tiny fertilized eggs settle down to the marsh bottom.

Although today, October sixteenth, I see little movement in the marsh, I suspect that life still courses below the surface. In September I paddled the marsh by moonlight, out beyond the muskrat lodge where the water deepens. A beaver towing an alder through a bar of reflected moonlight slapped his tail and dove. All around me, phantom midge larva rose toward the surface, twisting and snapping their thin, half-inch, transparent bodies. With one sweep of a small dip net, I caught several dozen and transferred them to a jar for a closer look. My flashlight revealed the dark air bladders at each end of the body, nothing more. At night, billions of phantom midges effervesce from the sediments to harpoon zooplankton (rotifers, mostly) on short, bristly antennae. To watch this I used my dissecting scope, for rotifers are smaller than dust motes.

Later that September, in a laboratory at Dartmouth College I glimpsed more of what happens below the surface of Lake Fairlee. Michele Dionne, a graduate student working on predator avoidance behavior, let me watch her experiment. She was studying the way damselfly nymphs position themselves on bulrushes to avoid the brightly colored pumpkinseed sunfish that methodically search each stalk for food.

She anchored sections of bulrush stems vertically to the bottom of six aquariums, four or eight to a tank, then blocked the sunfish from the stems with a Plexiglas panel and released damselfly nymphs into each tank. After the nymphs had swum to the stems, she freed the fish. When a pumpkinseed approached the bulrushes, all the nymphs crept in unison to the back sides of the stems. The sunfish almost never pursued them around the stem. The more nymphs per aquarium, the quicker they detected the sunfish and the quicker they sought cover, responding like a school of fish does, as a single organism. Tanks with only two or three nymphs had a higher rate of predation than tanks with four or eight. I flicked a bulrush, dislodging a nymph, and a pumpkin-seed arrived on the spot, devouring the twisting little insect. I left the college with an insight: Whenever my kayak paddle strikes a cattail stalk and dislodges an aquatic insect, an attentive sunfish probably gets a meal.

Now I paddle around the far end of the marsh, looking for whirligig beetles which just last week had gathered by the thousands to form several tight, oblong-shaped rafts. I count three; the rest must be in the mud, each with its bubble of air from which to breathe—an Aqualung of sorts, that is carried in a reservoir beneath its wing covers. I had drifted too close to that crowd of whirligigs last week. When I was twenty feet away, their collective engines revved. As I drifted closer, the raft appeared to explode. Beetles moved in all directions, spinning, darting, whirling on the surface like so many tiny bumper cars. I drifted away. They regrouped.

Flat and oval-shaped, a whittled-down version of a June beetle, the whirligig has divided eyes—one set sees above the surface, the other below—and short middle and hind legs that stroke the water fifty times per second for rapid propulsion. Plates at the end of these legs come together like the cupped hand of a swimmer on the power stroke, then open on the upstroke, allowing water to pass freely through. The long, thin front legs, ideal for grabbing insects off the surface, fold up and under the head, and a pair of short antennae rest at the surface to detect the slightest ripple.

So sensitive are the whirligig's antennae that a single beetle in a tightly packed raft, which may contain close to a quarter of a

13

million nervous beetles, never brushes against its neighbors, even when they are all moving helter-skelter. Much like a bat that reads returning sound waves in the air, the whirligig uses a form of echolocation to avoid collisions and to locate food. Its antennae read the echoes of its own ripples as they bounce back from objects in the water.

Whirligigs may congregate because their toxic secretions are thus more concentrated and more likely to repel predators. At night they disband to hunt along the surface film, sometimes commuting a mile away. Whenever I slap a mosquito, I drop it into the water and watch by flashlight as racing beetles head for dinner. When dawn comes, each whirligig joins other beetles in the area to form a new raft.

As the surface of Lake Fairlee cools, the heavier, cooler water sinks. Because water density increases as the temperature falls, warm water floats on a layer of colder, deeper water until it cools to 39.2 degrees Fahrenheit, the temperature at which water attains maximum density.

In summer, Lake Fairlee stratifies into three distinct zones: the top, or epilimnion; the middle, or metalimnion; and the bottom, or hypolimnion. Each zone circulates separately, and the winds of summer which agitate the surface cannot mix these layers. They remain as distinct as oil and vinegar. Diving through the epilimnion into the metalimnion is always a shock; the temperature suddenly drops ten to fifteen degrees Fahrenheit along an invisible boundary less than ten feet below the surface.

Of the three layers, the epilimnion—always in contact with air—is richest in oxygen and lowest in nutrients, which settle at the bottom of the lake. The hypolimnion gains all the nutrients that rain down during the summer but loses most of its oxygen to the enormous biomass of decomposers which respire in the sediments.

With the passing of summer and the coming of autumn, Lake Fairlee sheds its accumulated warmth as mist lifts high into the morning sky and drifts up the valley. Colder nights cause the surface water to cool and sink, so that the warm surface layer shrinks. Cool days yield to cool weeks, until the lake is a nearly uniform 39.2 degrees Fahrenheit. Below 39.2 degrees Fahrenheit water becomes less dense, and this cooler water floats. The lake stops circulating, overturn ends. Ice finally forms, generally by late December, and the lake is sealed off from the wind.

As I paddle offshore, Lake Fairlee continues its autumn overturn. I cannot see the overturn, of course, but I imagine that the flock of bufflehead, which arrived the other night from central Canada en route to some mid-Atlantic estuary for a winter respite, find plenty of aquatic insects and small fish dispersed at nearly all depths. The ducks idle in the middle of the lake. When I paddle toward them they dive, powered by large hind feet. Not far off, they surface—three males, mostly white, and four dull-colored birds, either females or the young of the year.

A beaver lodge, a misshapen mound of branches and trunks from sugar maples and yellow birches, packed with mud, extends from the shoreline like a half-submerged boulder. Last night's harvest floats in front, alder from the banks of Blood Brook, red oak from more than a mile away. One morning last summer as Casey and I drifted in front of the lodge, a beaver passed under my kayak, bubbles trailing from its fur. Fifty feet away, the beaver surfaced, swam parallel to the shoreline for a short way, then, arching slightly, slapped the water with its broad, flat, scaly tail, sending an arc of drops cascading into the morning air.

Beyond that beaver was another. Both animals alternately swam and dove, calling attention to each dive with a loud resounding slap. Neither stayed underwater longer than a couple of minutes or strayed far from the lodge. While we were watching the beavers, my kayak spun around to face the shore. Before we could turn back to the lake, a flash of brown halted me. A mink. Bounding from boulder to boulder, the mink jumped onto the beaver lodge, and stood straight up on its hind legs, watching us. Content that we were of little consequence, the animal sank to all fours, crossed the lodge and headed north along the bank toward the Blood Brook marshes, toward sunfish and bullfrogs and soft yearling turtles. We followed.

For a pleasant few minutes, while we focused on the mink, Lake Fairlee became wilder and more remote, a blue lake amid green hills. Gone were the developers who buy and build and sell and leave, without a sense of where they are. Gone were the high-horsepower motorboats, the water skiers, and their red and yellow slalom course. As we drifted too close, gone too was the mink.

Paddling beyond the lodge in October, I see two black-capped chickadees fill their bills with Lake Fairlee, tip their heads back, and swallow. Ahead of me lie the cattail marshes at the mouth of Middle Brook, the largest of the lake's seven tributaries, where a barred owl stole a friend's catfish as he reeled the fish in, and beyond that, the fork of the Ompompanoosuc's East Branch, a bold blue line on the topographical map. Compared to Blood Brook, East Branch is a torrent, draining sixty-five square miles of corrugated land—hills, plains and swamps—scored by brooks and spotted with lesser lakes. The river rushes over water-polished granite ledge.

With twilight closing in I turn back north, toward home. A skittish blue jay bathes, while noisy crows soar above. Four herring gulls and an immature black-legged kittiwake—a very rare inland visitor from the Arctic—eddy against a cranberry sky.

Remembering the Ice Age

To see tracks from the Ice Age, both actual and imagined, to sense Blood Brook and Lake Fairlee's past converging on the present, I join the ravens, which may or may not contemplate such things, high above the Blood Brook valley.

I am sitting in the front seat of a two-person glider, the pilot behind me, floating four thousand feet above the north end of Lake Fairlee. We drift with the wind, rising, sinking, gently and quietly, circling alone on currents, sailboating in the sky. Blood Brook valley lengthens below me, green and rumpled, a wildness to be indulged in, contemplated, savored. At its mouth, the brook splinters into innumerable channels, which saturate an alder-cattail marsh, then merge into a slightly deeper, lily-filled cove. Blood Brook's ramiform mouth emulates its headwaters, where, on the west side of Spaulding Hill, more than a dozen seeps and springs coalesce into a brook.

Just beyond the northeast corner of the lake, a seven-hundred-foot-deep gully cleaves the green, sloping hills. From a raven's perspective this is a prominent geologic feature, a great chop in a mound of living earth which I somehow miss while standing on firm ground. According to Vermont geologists, this "gap" was cut more than two million years ago by the late Ely River, an extinct, pre–Ice Age tributary to the Connecticut. It is the only large notch I can see between the Waits and the Ompompanoosuc rivers.

I imagine a turbulent, trout-filled Ely River—gouging, carving, pulverizing bedrock as it forms the future Lake Fairlee basin, as it takes the waters of Blood Brook and Middle Brook east along what is now an asphalt line, Route 244. In that epoch, hills thrust up raw and jagged, unplaned by glaciers. On an imagined topographical map of the Pleistocene epoch geologic survey, which I'll call the Ely River Quadrangle of 2.5 million years ago, the packed contour lines of Spaulding Hill and Bald Top show a steeper rise than they do today, perhaps a thousand feet above Blood Brook, which is visible as only a skinny blue line. Such a map might bear a strong likeness to a patch of modern Rocky Mountain Idaho.

From my vantage point just beneath the clouds, I see the fossil-course of Blood Brook: south down Bloodbrook Road, east on 244, around the north end of Lake Fairlee, through Ely River pass (home now to droning vehicles instead of purling water), then south on Route 5 along the Connecticut River, where cows graze the ancient delta.

Before the first of four waves of Pleistocene glaciers bulldozed Blood Brook valley, a lower branch of the Ompompanoosuc River turned north and hijacked the Ely River near Post Mills, redirecting its flow westward, eventually joining the Connecticut about ten miles south of the Ely River's former delta. Blood Brook and Middle Brook with the Ely River, then emptied to the south.

Gradually the old drainage route lapsed, and the Ely River pass became dry, a victim of restless, unsettled topography.

About fourteen thousand years ago, the retreating glacier left a stagnant block of ice in the Ely River valley. Sand and gravel washed in, piled up eighty feet deep against the southwest edge of the rotten ice, and held its waters back to form a classic kettle hole lake—Lake Fairlee, incarcerated in the imprint of an ancient flowage, sum of ice, landscape, and fate.

Looking across the watershed, I imagine a time about a thousand years after Lake Fairlee first appeared, when ice and glacial debris blocked the flow of the Connecticut River near Middletown, Connecticut, about one hundred and fifty miles below Lake Fairlee. The big river backed up to Burke, Vermont, flooding its own valley and the connected lowlands, including the Ely River pass, Lake Fairlee, and halfway up Blood Brook and Middle Brook. The river system was transformed into a giant lake—its chemistry, biology, and shoreline changed from that of swift to standing water. Even the principal species of aquatic insects must have shifted with the new regime. Called Lake Hitchcock, the ephemeral glacial lake resembles a squashed yellow centipede on the Surficial Geologic Map of Vermont, its appendages reaching up our modern river valleys.

Gliding on in our airborne boat, we see a run of round green domes southeast of Lake Fairlee—Potato Hill, Ely Mountain, Houghton Hill. From my kitchen on a cool morning last June, I watched the mist rise off the lake and fill the valley, much as Lake Hitchcock must have done. And suddenly I realized that the tops of familiar local hills must have once been islands in the glacial lake. As they emerged from the mist, I saw the specters of mammoths and mastodons stalked by both Paleolithic hunters and by an unknown, unforgiving future.

This geologic metamorphosis was also temporary. The earth

and ice dam broke. Valleys drained. Rivers and brooks thinned. Islands became hilltops again. Shallow ponds dried to meadows. Freed-up northern New England water must have poured into the Long Island Sound with unimaginable force. Then, a second dam at Turners Falls, Massachusetts, backed up the water again, to create Lake Upham. Finally, about ten thousand years ago, when that dam ruptured and Lake Upham discharged its holdings, the Connecticut River flowed freely, and modern Lake Fairlee emerged, still tied to the hills by geocentric streams, a great blue basin in an otherwise greening valley. Silt and clay from the bottom of Lake Hitchcock, and sand and gravel from its old shore, freshly exposed and glacially minted, would support first tundra then forest.

Catching a tongue of air deflecting off Bald Top, spiraling higher into the firmament, the glider carries us beyond Lake Fairlee, across Route 244. A turkey vulture passes below, wings cocked obliquely, rocking like a toy kite. I see Blood Brook valley, broadly U-shaped. A wall of brown sand, perhaps the remnant of a prehistoric beach, stands above a pasture; a vestige of Lake Hitchcock, the sand hosts nesting turtles. On dark nights in June, painted turtles excavate in open sand, often along the flank of the wall. At dawn, snapping turtles, even more prehistoric than the old beach, dig in the sparsely vegetated flats that run south toward the road. From three thousand feet, I see Blood Brook descend through the glacially widened valley, twice swelling into a series of beaver ponds—one near the brook's lower end, the other more than a mile to the north. White, barkless sticks on the lodge of the lower-pond beavers glint in the sun. Recent ancestors of these beavers probably dispersed upstream from the lake as generations have done since the withdrawal of the last glacier.

The lodge of the upper-pond beavers, probably descendants of the lower-pond family, is screened by a mesh of shrubs. Even when I stand at the edge of their pond, I cannot always see their lodge, but I have seen freshly cut aspens and alders and an elderly yet fully flowered apple.

Late last April, a pair swam upstream, entered our pond, and stayed for a few days, cavorting in full view of Linny and Casey, who picnicked on the shoreline. By the time I came home from California, they were gone. They left behind a flotilla of debarked aspen branches and a crude, stick-domed lodge, which they visited again several weeks later.

From the air, it's possible to look across Spaulding Hill: to the northeast, I see the White Mountains, their peaks still white with June snow; to the northwest, Mount Mansfield, capped by a bit of arctic tundra. Looking south, I see Blood Brook's waters merge with the flow from a dozen other valleys to feed the East Branch of the Ompompanoosuc, then the Connecticut River, before coursing to sea. I see a great green sprawl, dendritic drainages from valley to valley to the horizon, a three-dimensional map.

Land is the manifestation of its memory. As the climate grew warmer, Blood Brook's tundra was gradually replaced by spruce, fir, and larch, whose descendents still cast pollen from the edges of nearby peatlands, themselves remnants of shallow Ice Age lakes that slowly filled with sediment. Peatlands are a type of wetland that abound in accumulated organic soils. In them deposition exceeds decomposition. Like Mount Washington's Alpine Garden, peatlands are remainders of a boreal past and akin to the present-day Canadian north, seemingly out of place in an otherwise summer-green woods. Sequestered in cool pockets, bound by an evergreen noose that is slowly closing, the peatland, bogs, fens, and cedar swamps are ephemeral.

One Memorial Day I visited a northern white cedar swamp, an hour's drive north of Blood Brook. I saw the sun while driving, but by the time I reached Barnet, it hid behind mounds of clouds which fell away, one behind the other, like a fading roll of hills. I parked and entered the woods. The cool air smelled like a cedar chest. A Canada warbler flitted through the deep, conifer shade. On a mulch hummock I soon found calypso, one of the rarest and most beautiful orchids in northern New England, and the reason for my trip.

Gently, I fingered calypso. Two lateral petals and three sepals, with five tapering magenta fingers, radiated from the cap of an inflated, slipper-shaped orchid. The top of the lip, white and yellow, dotted with purple, spread into an apron that curled at the edges and was cleft at the tip. Brown-purple lines streaked arrow-like down the slipper's side, pointing toward a prominent tuft of yellow hairs at the base of the apron. An unsuspecting bumblebee would enter, mistake the hairs for pollen, and, after a futile attempt to collect them, would force her way into the slipper to search for food. Instead of nectar, two sticky pollen balls would be firmly glued to her head.

If calypso is to be pollinated, the bee must repeat her mistake, look for pollen grains in another flower, and then finding none must enter the slipper where the viscous surface of the pistil or stigma scrapes the pollen from her head, fertilizing the orchid. Once the bumblebee learns that calypso offers no edible pollen or nectar, she will stop returning. Which is to say, this elfin orchid depends on recently metamorphosed and totally inexperienced bumblebees, the naive bees of spring, to complete its reproductive cycle. Pollinated, the sepals and petals brown and fall, and the inferior ovary, enclosed at the base of the lip, produces a crop of dustlike seeds. Each seed contains only enough food to start germination. In order to grow a seed must come in contact with a specific soil fungus that will supply nutrients to the developing embryo. Without the proper fungus, it dies. Shy and beautiful as the sea nymph in Homer's *Odyssey,* calypso gambles against great odds, casting hundreds of thousands of seeds across the cedar glade. Very few germinate, and fewer still survive, for calypso grows in only four locations in Vermont, a messenger from another age.

Ice Age mammals fire my imagination. Shaggy Scotch highlander cattle and woolly winter horses look like they've just stepped off the wall of a cave painting. They evoke images of the Pleistocene: bands of mammoths and mastodons, trunks, tusks, and floppy ears, ranging across a northern landscape. This is Blood Brook, perhaps ten thousand years ago, when tundra reached down from the Green Mountains to the edge of the emerging spruce woods.

In 1848, railroad construction workers unearthed a pile of large fossil bones in Mount Holly, Vermont. Renowned Harvard zoologist and geologist Louis Agassiz identified them as belonging to a woolly mammoth, the Ice Age elephant whose remains are more often associated with Siberia and Alaska. This discovery suggests that Vermont was once bleak and windy, an arctic outpost, peopled by wandering nomads who followed roving herds of Ice Age mammals north as the glaciers waned.

More information has been gathered about woolly mammoths than any other extinct species. Fossil ivory hunters, who comb the subarctic for curved mammoth tusks, have excavated entire carcasses frozen in the permafrost, and dissection has shed light on the animals' seasonal diet: grasses, sedges, poppies, and ferns in the summer; willow, birch, and larch in the winter. One intact mammoth, discovered in Siberia at the end of the nineteenth century, had died so suddenly in a glacial crevice that it held twenty-four pounds of food in its mouth, and much more in its stomach.

As days grew colder and shorter, a woolly mammoth began to store an enormous amount of fat to buffer it against the arctic winter. Sinuses on the top of its head, on either side of a large ridge of pinched-up bone called the sagittal crest, filled with fat, hence the massive cranial knob. Behind its neck another huge mound of seasonal fat developed, much like a camel's hump. The mound and knob of fat were hedges against diminished food resources; by the time spring arrived and grazing was again profitable, a woolly mammoth had metabolized its store of fat.

American mastodons, which browsed Blood Brook's conifers at about the same time that woolly mammoths grazed its tundra, left more fossil bones than any other creature that ever lived. Buried remains have been recovered from bogs, preserved by the acidic waters. One mastodon had five bushels of conifer twigs packed inside its rib cage, and numerous others were found with food-impacted molars that showed signs of a preference for spruce and hemlock needles, trees which still grow on Spaulding Hill. Some mastodons had pine pitch jammed between the cusps of their molars; it is no wonder that paleontologists suggest tooth decay and pyorrhea were common.

Brittle, broken mastodon tusks dug up from clay deposits disintegrate in air, but those preserved in bogs reveal that mastodons were either right- or left-tusked. When a pair of long, straight tusks are found together, one is invariably shorter than the other, which suggests that these animals used one to the exclusion of the other for breaking branches. Woolly mammoth tusks, which grew out and up and curled back in, plowed snow from the surface of the ground and show no signs of preference for right or left scraping.

Even the social structure of these animals can be deduced from the fossil record, which helps us visualize a creature that was a lot more than an eating machine. I recently visited the Mammoth Site of Hot Spring, South Dakota, where the remains of more than a hundred Columbian mammoths (a close grassland relative of the woolly mammoth) have been found. After slaking their thirst in a prairie sinkhole, the animals either drowned or starved when the sides of the basin proved too slippery to climb. Most of the fossils are those of young adult males, the counterparts of human teenagers. Based on comparisons with the social structure of African elephants, to whom they are closely related, biologists say that young males were probably driven from their herds, and that naiveté led them into what eventually became their mausoleums. Young adult females stayed with the herd, juveniles and infants stayed with their mothers, and adult males were too experienced to venture into a risky sinkhole.

I can almost sense the herds along Blood Brook, roaming, feeding, socializing at the dawn of human memory. These enormous mammals must have been a powerful force in the evolution of the plants on which they fed. The press of prehistory can still be detected in some of these plants.

Paleontologists believe that the giant ground sloth, an extinct Ice Age behemoth that sat upright and pulled branches into its mouth, exerted such enormous pressure on incipient desert vegetation that ocotillo thorns and cactus spines developed as self-defense. These adaptations persist, though sloths have been extinct for more than six thousand years. Pawpaw, a hardwood of the southern Appalachian flood plains, produces a five-inch cylindrical fruit that suggests a banana. After feeding the brownish fruit to several woodland omnivores (a raccoon and an opossum, I believe) as well as an elephant, a biologist discovered that pawpaw seeds germinated best in the manure pile that the elephant supplied. Then, gazing into evolution's crystal ball, he speculated that the pawpaw, the lone member of a tropical family of plants to have immigrated into the temperate zone, evolved its large, sugary fruit to entice mastodons to disperse its seeds.

Where are the evolutionary footprints to be found in the Northeast?

My vision is not sensitive enough to see the mark mammoths and mastodons left on Blood Brook's vegetation, but I may have found them roaming the outback of an Western Abenaki myth. Can these giants have survived in Paleolithic stories, their images indelibly painted in the mind, sharp and bright as those rendered on the walls of the caves of the Dordogne? Could stories have been passed down through the centuries—via what Abenaki author Joseph Bruchac calls "the long memory"—into the age of Woodland Indians, a journey of some eight thousand years? In "Snowy Owl and the Great White Hare," a tale Bruchac retells, the Ktchiawaasak—huge, mound-shaped beasts, each with two long teeth—drank the People's springs and lakes dry and squashed the scouts until Snowy Owl tricked them into falling over, then shot them in the soles of their feet with ivory arrowheads sprung from an ivory bow.

That American mastodons and woolly mammoths survived to the fringe of recorded history, brushing against the very species of trees which populate Blood Brook valley, thrills me. They likely knew the lilt of the brook, the song of the chickadee, the drumming of the grouse. And likely, too, I've walked where they walked, sat where they sat, peed where they peed, and breathed the same cool air that once filled their enormous lungs.

Tales of Tadpoles

Attracted by their effervescent babble, I go to our pond each spring to watch the sexual congress of frogs and toads. On the first warm, rainy, April night, wood frogs come out of their hibernacula in the forest soil to breed in the water, and the north end of the valley grows urgent with their clamorous voices. Responding to my footfalls along the shoreline, frogs fall silent. The cooler the air temperature, the longer they will remain so. Below forty-five degrees Fahrenheit, I just watch from a distance, for if I approach too close, the chorus may take hours to revive. Above sixty degrees Fahrenheit, only the frogs closest to me stop singing; then, encouraged by their neighbors' voices, they quickly rejoin the chorus.

Frogs lead me back to the steamy Carboniferous period, to the swamps of 300 million years ago, from which adventurous amphibians first crept (with some trepidation, I suspect) out of the water. That amphibians were capable of making such a radical change is not too surprising. Their own immediate ancestors, lobe-finned fish, had the requisite tools and were preadapted to take the proper steps; lobe-fins already had lungs for gulping air at the surface of stagnant water and thick limbs for waddling over pond bottoms. Seasonal droughts seem to have motivated lobe-fins to crawl down shriveling stream beds in search of water. Those with the stoutest, most functional limbs survived. As Alfred Sherwood Romer, the preeminent comparative anatomist, noted, early amphibians were "little more than four-legged fish."

The journey of those primitive, froglike animals out of the organic bath and ultimately into the trees was a grand evolutionary experiment that eventually resulted in reptiles and birds and mammals, then primates, *Pithecanthropus* and *Australopithecus*, *Homo erectus* and *Homo sapiens*.

A more conservative crowd than some of their ancestors, frogs and toads remained wed to wetlands, returning each spring to breed. After watching their mating rituals, I decided to consider the tadpoles. I wanted to recognize the species that hatch in our pond and follow their metamorphoses from egg to froglet, to see how various species coexist. Where and how do they feed? Who are their enemies? As a self-employed naturalist, I had lots of time to spend by the pond, listening to the rhythms of its tribes and watching Casey begin to mesh slowly with Blood Brook valley, the landscape of his boyhood.

At almost two years old, Casey was already admiring tadpoles; he would drop wiffle balls in their aquarium and bid them good night before going to sleep. I expected him to be thoroughly dazzled by their transformation into froglets. One May, before his third birthday, we found American toad tadpoles hatching five days after we had seen their eggs being laid. Tens of thousands of black tadpoles covered the rocks, water weeds, and lines of disintegrating jelly that had recently held their eggs. Each tadpole hung tail down, fastened to the weeds or rocks or jelly by facial suckers, two raised patches of skin near the mouth which secrete a sticky substance.

Their bellies distended, newts worked the shoreline and feasted, snapping up tadpoles one after the other until they could eat no more. Seventeen newts, some feeding, some resting, all fat with tadpoles, lounged in the May sunshine. For days, even weeks, they had fed on the hatchlings without making a noticeable dent in their numbers. Each day mats of toad tadpoles gathered in the shallows and blackened our footprints in the sand, while another new hatch clung by suction to anything that didn't move.

Floating above the bottom-dwelling black tadpoles, a shoal of fawn-colored wood frog tadpoles idled just below the surface. More than an inch long, these had hatched several weeks earlier and were by now able swimmers, powered by their finned tails. As I watched the water, I realized that the frogs outnumbered the toads. Head to tail, wood frog tadpoles milled in such astronomical numbers that I find it easiest to describe them by the surface area they covered: a hundred square feet, five hundred square feet, or maybe even more. Unpredictable and unexpected, like a banner crop of raspberries; this was proving a cardinal spring for spawning wood frogs.

Endless herds of tadpoles, plump and brown, brought to mind aerial views of wildebeests migrating across the Serengeti; they were tended by newts—the lions and hyenas of the aquatic plain— who sprawled at the surface, eating and digesting. Tadpoles seemed to know when a newt wasn't hunting; they simply opened their school to let it swim through, like zebras and wildebeests accommodating a passing lion. A stalking newt was avoided, yet only by those tadpoles closest to it. The other tadpoles just beguiled time, loafing at the surface, warmed by the sun, apparently oblivious to the peril of their neighbors.

After more than an hour, I finally saw a newt catch a big frog tadpole. At this stage in their development a single wood frog tadpole is as big as at least ten toad tadpoles. So large was its meal that the newt took several minutes to swallow the tadpole, and the victim stuck out, cigarlike, from the newt's mouth.

The tadpoles grew rapidly. A week later, although newts still swam among them, the wood frog tadpoles were too big to eat.

To encourage Casey's interest, I set up an aquarium on our porch, added both American toad and wood frog tadpoles, and waited for the magic to start.

Every morning and every afternoon, we inspected our tenants for a sign of metamorphosis. Any sign would do, a hind leg breaking through the base of a tadpole's tail, or a vanishing tail, absorbed and redistributed to another part of the body, or a tadpole at the surface gulping air to satisfy its incipient lungs. Patiently, I looked for signs that they were becoming frogs, but nothing appeared to be happening. They were a watched pot that wouldn't boil.

Although the tadpoles in the pond also showed no visible sign of metamorphosis, they were at least three times bigger than their captive counterparts. Food and temperature were the keys to the problem. Since our aquarium sat on the screened porch, it was subjected to the vagaries of the weather, and since it held only three gallons of water, its temperature fluctuated more than that of the pond: it was warm during the day, but cool at night. Being cold-blooded, tadpoles grow more quickly in warm water, more slowly in cool water. The pond, a larger and more stable environment, husbands heat, retaining warmth at night and thus permitting the wild tadpoles to feed and grow at a higher metabolic rate than captive ones.

And of course the pond contains more nutritious food. Although they do scavenge carcasses of frogs and other soft-bodied animals that have settled into the muck, frog tadpoles subsist mainly on algae, pond weeds, and the veneer of bacteria which coats old, water-logged cattail stalks.

When Casey and I visited the pond, thousands of wood frog tadpoles were gathered in the shallows at the north end. There were so many of them in such a small area that the water roiled. They wiggled and thrashed at the surface, feeding. Unavoidably stepping on tadpoles, I waded into the muck to have a closer look. When I reached the midst of the feeding frenzy, I stopped, kneeled down, and watched them rasp off slimy coats of bacteria from the broken cattail stalks and rotting leaves that had drifted into that corner of the pond.

I picked up several strands of cattails and returned to the aquarium. As soon as Casey dropped the cattails in water, the tadpoles stopped eating the blue-green algae off the aquarium wall and began feasting on their new food. With the aid of a small magnifying glass, we watched the expressionless tadpole faces, their lips puckered in mock conversation. Encircled by a fleshy papillary fringe, which identifies the nature of potential food, each black horny mouth flexed and relaxed, flexed and relaxed. The extent of the papillary fringe aids in identifying unknown tadpoles: the toad tadpole's fringe is incomplete on the bottom, looking somewhat like mutton-chop sideburns, whereas on wood frog tadpoles the fringe meets at the bottom, a Vandyke, giving the tadpole a rather cosmopolitan look.

Impatient with the pace of their development, a few days later I swapped our runty tadpoles for a few robust, free-swimming ones from the pond. Still no legs. I did find something worth noting, however: a tadpole is not just a round head with a long tail. Beneath the layers of transparent body skin, I saw the contours of a frog: angled face and streamlined, thin mouth; swelling eyes like new potatoes; rounded, blunt torso.

To tell the truth, I was a little disappointed in this discovery. With it the mystery of amphibian metamorphosis has receded into a series of slow, gradual changes that transforms one creature into another, mostly visible in stages if one cares to look closely. I would have preferred my tadpoles, like caterpillars in cocoons, to emerge as frogs suddenly, magically.

That spring I worked occasionally with John Douglas, a portrait photographer with a quick wit, the ability to coax a smile from a stone, a serious interest in chocolate cake, and a lifelong, devotion to the Boston Red Sox. Tall, sturdy, bearded John co-leads nature tours with me; because he is a selectman for Vershire, Vermont, while traveling he often conducts town business from desert telephone booths.

John is not, however, a soil scientist. Neither am I. We set up a thirty-gallon aquarium, adding to the water several dozen wood frog tadpoles; caddisfly larva; backswimmer and damselfly nymphs; two newts; two large, incorrigible green frog tadpoles with robust hind legs; roundworms beyond counting; plus seven sedge stalks and three cattail stalks. This aquarium was to be our pond's "eye," a chance for us to combine talents and create pictures of life below the surface without getting our feet wet.

We poured in the sediment, a half-filled five-gallon bucket of unconsolidated pond bottom which I had lugged over a steep, wet, meadow while wearing shower clogs. Sweating and winded, knees green with grass stains, bellowing for the door to be opened, I had reached the screened porch where both John and the aquarium waited—one filled with water, the other overflowing with laughter. We watched silt mushroom from the bottom like the cloud above an explosion, eclipsing everything in the tank. We could see nothing but swirling brown: gone were the tadpoles, the newts, the insects, the plants.

Two hours later, after lunch at the local diner, the aquarium was darker than the streets of Varanasi. And two hours after that, after a refreshing nap, the aquarium was still opaque. The next morning, a couple of tadpoles pressed against the glass, the first signs of life I had noticed since the muck was poured. Somewhat encouraged, I stepped closer to assess the situation. No light passed through the back of the aquarium; no line demarcated the bottom sediment from what was still suspended in the water. Those tadpoles that swam an inch beyond the glass were reduced to shadows.

Five days later faint lines of green sedge resolved themselves in the colloid haze. Three thin, erect, white worms undulated from the bottom like belly dancers. Now, three or four inches from the glass, tadpoles looked like tadpoles, not shadows, and the red spots of a newt floating near the surface were visible. A suggestion of sunlight had advanced through the back of the aquarium.

But the water never completely cleared. Never. The suspended particles, remnants of clay-bottomed Lake Hitchcock, were much too small to settle anywhere within the range of our patience, and constant agitation by the troops of amphibians, insects and worms kept the broth in motion.

Too bad, because the tadpoles soon began to transmogrify. Their hind legs sprouted, front legs pushed out against opercula like beans elbowing through the topsoil, tails and intestines shortened, faces narrowed, gills disappeared, eyes swelled, mouths widened, black baby lips fell off.

I didn't have to see into the aquarium to know what was going on. From my vantage point on the hill, I watched wood frog tadpoles rising vertically to the surface to gulp air. The pond looked as though it was being hit by a hard, steady, but arrhythmic summer rain. Disparate, concentric rings spread everywhere.

I wondered how I could have missed such a mass transformation last year or any year. The pond, with its tens of thousands of wood frog tadpoles, and the thirty-gallon aquarium, with its dozen, finally boiled with urgency.

Transformed by tepid pond water, heated under the full press of the July sun, a galaxy of dime-sized wood frogs assembled along the shoreline. Those with long tails stayed close to the pond or swam at the surface, stroking the water with their four small feet. Testing their new limbs against gravity, froglets popped at Casey's feet. Most returned to the pond, but some hopped boldly on, toward the meadow, the willows, the dark green pine woods.

Thousands of fawn-colored froglets that are, except for tail nubbins, miniature replicas of their parents, attracted the attention of more than just curious naturalists. From my studio deck, I saw blue jays hopping around the pond. With the aid of binoculars, I watched from a distance and speculated on their success. Every time they bent their heads, they plucked a froglet. While the jays harvested froglets in the sedges, backswimmers harvested froglets in the water, and inch-and-a-half-long green frogs—themselves only days away from their own tadpole stage—sat fixed on the shoreline, waiting for the moveable feast. For Casey, slashing the pond with his dip net, catching wood frogs was no more difficult than picking strawberries.

Backswimmers are half-inch long, oval-shaped aquatic insects. As their name implies, they swim upside down, hanging down from the surface tension at a forty-five-degree angle. Their reverse shading—light on their backs, dark on their bellies—makes them almost invisible from below or above. Powered by long hind legs, they jitter through the depths, abruptly changing direction whenever their sensitive abdominal hairs detect the slightest vibration. They have macabre feeding habits and insatiable appetites for tadpoles and other slow moving, soft-bodied prey.

Like other true bugs—I mean taxonomic bugs, members of the insect order *Hemiptera*, not the catchall category for any small, unknown insect—backswimmers have piercing and sucking mouthparts. They hook onto a tadpole from underneath, jab their hypodermic mouths into its flesh, pump in digestive juices that dissolve the tadpole's innards, and then sip away, so the tadpole deflates like a leaky balloon. Only a loose bag of skin is left. Idling in the kayak, we watched a backswimmer stalk a floating frog. It glided under the frog and touched it. The frog kicked forward several inches, then stopped. The backswimmer followed. Again, it touched the frog, and again the frog kicked forward. On the backswimmer's fifth pass, the frog hopped tentatively onto land.

I paddled on. Four-legged tadpoles with inch-long tails sculled at the surface, while less developed ones rose vertically, filled their nascent lungs with air, then dove back into the brown shadowless depths, leaving a tiny, bubble at the surface. Scores of froglets piled forward onto the banks, the emanations of an ancient contingency where preadapted lobe-finned fish left their drying streambeds. Three froglets hitched rides on the bow of the kayak.

A week later, in mid-July, the surface of the pond was an amalgam of organic debris, trashed with moth wings left over from hungry tree swallows or dragonflies; spent midges and mayflies; and exoskeletons from damselflies and dragonflies blown off the cattails. A rose chaffer treaded water. I slugged a horsefly and dropped her into the brew.

Sweat poured from me as I paddled. The afternoon was hot and sticky, like summer in south Florida. A green frog twanged. A robin caroled from the pines, and beyond the willows, Blood

Brook hummed a cool song. Blackflies slipped into the body cavity of the kayak, crawled up our legs, chewed on our ankles, and
then crawled out again, bloated. I plucked the nape of Casey's
shirt, driving mosquitoes from his back.

What if stream beds had not begun to dry up 300 million
years ago? Would lobe-finned fish still "walk" on the bottom of
tropical ponds? Would vertebrate evolution have diverged along
unknown, unimagined lineages? Would Earth support conscious
thought?

I looked at Casey. What if Linny and I had not merged with
wine nearly six years ago?

Turtles in Books
and Bogs

South to the lake. South down the valley, past the ninety-one-year-old farmer, the basket maker, the candy maker, and the undertaker (who are all the same person) to a stretch of open water where laughter carries for a mile. From the hemlock stands along our driveway, past the dust and the ruts of the cow pastures, to where summer-green cattails give way to white-flowered lilies and pink-flowered smartweed, where colored turtles bask on logs and monster snappers plod through the shallows.

One morning in late June, I secured my kayak on the car, drove to the lake, and parked at the place where Blood Brook enters a culvert and passes under the road. The flood plain is flat and sandy. Three feet off the road a snapping turtle was digging her nest, a mere scrape in the sand. I had been tracking her for some time. As I stretched motionless in the grass, the nonchalant mother turtle methodically laid twenty-seven round, white, leathery eggs—one at a time, at three to four minute intervals. Her pebble-sized brain was fixed on the task; her primal yellow eyes stared straight ahead, unblinking. After each egg dropped into the nest, she delicately positioned it with her long-clawed hind feet. When she was finished, before she turned around, she covered her work with sand, packed it solid with her hind feet, then lumbered back to the brook. She would never again see those eggs again.

To predict the sex of a snapping turtle's eggs, you need a thermometer. The temperature of the nest, two-thirds of the way through the nine to twelve weeks of incubation, determines the embryos' sex: eighty-four degrees Fahrenheit or hotter produces females; eighty degrees Fahrenheit or cooler produces mostly males. In between, either sex may develop. Since eggs at the top of the nest are warmer than those at the bottom, mostly females hatch from the top eggs, and mostly males hatch from the bottom. Somehow this arrangement must produce a balance of males and females, for snapping turtles have been around for a long time. Relics from the Mesozoic era, they are among the most primitive of living reptiles.

During mild September weather, hatchling snapping turtles emerge from their nest and crawl straight to the marsh; harsh weather keeps them in the nest until spring, either in or out of their shell. On a crisp October afternoon I returned to the nest I'd found earlier and dug into it, uncovering scraps of eggshells curled along the edges, but no whole eggs or turtles. A skunk had prowled nearby, teased the sand with its claws and left some scat, now dried. Had the turtles hatched, I wondered? I broke apart the scat: apple skin and apple seeds, beetle parts, pieces of yellow jackets, but no snapping turtles. Then I checked for road kills: the greater the number, the larger the exodus. Three dark spots on the paved road: two dimensional baby turtles, flattened by traffic. Some turtles, at least, had hatched.

Once in the marsh, turtles pass the winter tucked in the muck, insulated from the frost by a layer of ice and snow. What little oxygen they need is absorbed from the water through the linings of the throat and cloaca.

Winter in the nest is less predictable. One year 80 percent of the hatchlings might perish; the next all will survive. Several years ago, a cold and snowless December destroyed any turtles that stayed in the nest. The difference between life and death is snow depth. Deep snow insulates the turtles. Without it, they turn to stone; ice crystals rupture their cells.

But what about before the snow, when the ground freezes six or seven inches deep, how then do hatchling snapping turtles survive? Turtles don't produce glycerol, an alcohol synthesized by insects and terrestrial hibernating frogs which lowers their freezing point (and which is also used in several brands of commercial antifreeze). Instead, they supercool, a quirk of physical science pioneered by plants and later demonstrated for a 1950s television audience by Mr. Wizard, the evangelical physicist.

Water normally freezes at thirty-two degrees Fahrenheit. Yet hatchling snapping turtles have molecules in their systems which inhibit ice crystal formation by disturbing the molecular bonding and preventing a rigid lattice structure from forming. In this state, if touched by an ice crystal, a turtle immediately freezes. I remember watching Mr. Wizard demonstrate the principle, lowering the freezing point of distilled water well below thirty-two degrees. He then added an ice crystal to his experiment and produced an instant block of ice. In the absence of an ice crystal, water can be supercooled to as low as minus forty degrees Fahrenheit.

Through the internal mechanism that lowers the freezing point of their bodies to seventeen degrees Fahrenheit, hatchling snapping turtles survive November without ice crystals piercing their cells. However, a frigid, snowless December like that of 1989 brings disaster.

Painted turtles, which also hatch from sand nests near Blood Brook, take winter adaptation one step further than snapping turtles; they have "freeze tolerance," the ability to survive partial freezing. Although up to 53 percent of their extracellular fluids may have frozen, hatchling painted turtles that have overwintered in the nest can still thaw and crawl away, making them the only known turtle with this capacity.

One morning in late June several years ago, more than an inch and a quarter of rain fell in less than two hours. Rain found a route into our home through the crack at a dining room windowsill, topped off Casey's green plastic swimming pool, filled our nearly empty hummingbird feeder, and flooded tiger beetle and eastern sand wasp burrows along the sandy margins of our patio. Blood Brook turned into Big Muddy, the driveway into the Borrego Badlands, and the valley into a rainforest.

Before the first raindrop struck, while the wind gathered power and the sky darkened ominously, purple finches, rose-breasted grosbeaks, American goldfinches, and blue jays fled from the front yard maple and disappeared into the surrounding woods. After the rain, Blood Brook ran brown and wide, gushing through a nearby stone wall with the force of a fire hydrant. Watching all this torrent, I thought about the painted turtles. Had their nests been washed out?

For the past three years, around the summer solstice, a painted turtle has crossed Route 244 in late afternoon to lay eggs. And for the past three years, I've picked her up and taken her home with me to photograph and to show to Casey.

She prefers the marsh muck to our Mexican tile floor. All night long, her plastron claps the tiles. Since her peregrinations keep me awake, I move her out to the porch, where she thumps through the night against a less resonant pine floor. After a day or two in captivity, I let her go, always at twilight, and always in the sandy loam near the mouth of Blood Brook.

Painted turtles dig nests in sandy soil, sometimes more than a mile from water, in the late afternoon or early evening. After laying six to ten eggs, they make their way back to water. Snapping turtles lay at dawn or shortly after, and rarely stay out past 10:00 A.M. I do not know why these turtles, both of which bask in the sun, avoid laying their eggs in the middle of the day.

Mammalian turtle egg connoisseurs—skunks and raccoons, for instance—are hard to outwit: they're nocturnal, hunt with their noses, and are adept at finding buried food. Perhaps, though, the turtles avoid diurnal, egg-eating birds like crows and ravens and gulls, which have excellent memories and hunt by sight.

Biologist J. David Henry, author of *Red Fox: The Catlike Canid*, believes that foxes bury their cache so that crows and jays can't find it. It may be that turtles do likewise. After covering their eggs, I've watched painted and snapping turtles pat down and smooth the sand with their plastrons until almost all traces of the nest have disappeared. Unless I flag the spot, I may lose track of a nest site.

On the afternoon of the deluge, I thought of our painted turtle acquaintance. If she had dug her nest too close to the sandy shores of Blood Brook, a wall of thick, brown water would certainly have swamped the site and drowned the eggs, washing away an entire year's worth of reproductive effort. Unlike birds, turtles never renest the year their eggs are destroyed.

After the rain stopped, Casey and I drove down the valley to the lake. Provisioned with snacks, a bottle of seltzer, a pair of binoculars, and a notebook, we launched the kayak in the marsh. Casey searched for drifting tennis balls escaped from the children's camps, while I searched for turtles. I have counted as many as fourteen painted turtles basking in the marsh at one time. Just after 6:00 P.M. the sun flooded the marsh in yellow light. Facing the brilliance, we saw glistening oval-shaped lily pads, black on the radiant water. Accented by milk-white flowers, lines of overlapping pads curled into the lake. Cattails glowed yellow-green. Turning to put the sun behind us, we saw the marsh as a weave of greens: light green, dark green, olive green, brownish green. Above the marsh swallows trolled for flies, while slow cedar waxwings chased even slower moths. Their long, barbed legs dangling like brushes, dragonflies combed midges and mosquitoes from the air. A luminous blue damselfly landed on the bow of kayak, rode with us for several strokes of the paddle and then fluttered away.

A redwing screamed. A kingfisher rattled.

Three painted turtles basking on a waterlogged elm trunk craned their yellow-striped necks at our approach. Taking no chances, the biggest turtle, whose carapace was as long as my hand, slipped into the shallow water. I paddled closer. The two small ones leaned forward, then plunged in. Casey laughed.

A couple of minutes later, the big painted turtle poked its head from between a mat of lily pads. As we floated closer, the turtle cocked its head, tracking the kayak. By now, both small painted turtles had climbed back onto the log. I headed for the elm. As soon as my paddle slit the water, the big turtle vanished, and the smaller ones snapped to attention. As the kayak grazed the log, both turtles hit the water with a splash. I followed the turtles by watching the lily pads and water smartweed. As the turtles plowed through the tangled stems, the pads moved. When the pads stopped moving, I knew a turtle had stopped to rest on the soft bottom, four inches below the surface. After several minutes, the big turtle headed for open water trailed by a cloud of muck which rose at its heels, but the smaller turtles stayed put.

Casey fell asleep as I edged the kayak behind the log, directly over the turtles, one of which panicked, bumping stems and shaking pads along its way. The other one held its position, screened from view by a big lily pad. As the kayak drifted past the lily, the turtle's bright neck and legs looked even brighter against the muck. Reaching into the water behind the lily, I grabbed the turtle. A young painted turtle has a proportionally larger head than an adult and cannot withdraw entirely into its thinner, softer shell, yet this one did not even attempt to retreat. Feet stroking, neck extended, he treaded air, pinioned in my hand. I put him on the floor of the kayak and, skidding past Casey's legs, the turtle raced into the darkness of the bow, toenails scratching fiberglass.

For two weeks the painted turtle lived on our porch in an aquarium, eating minced worms and sunbathing in the morning, three miles away from its home in Spaulding Hill sediments that had been ferried to the lake by Blood Brook.

To learn more about an animal or plant, I can go to the field or go to the library. Each has its intrinsic rewards. In the field—the marsh, in this case—I arouse my senses, silence my mind, exercise my body, and provoke my appetite. With each trip, I learn something new.

On March 16, 1852, Thoreau wrote in his journal, "The library is a wilderness of books. . . . I saw that while we are clearing the forest in our westward progress, we are accumulating a forest of books in our rear, as wild and unexplored as any of nature's primitive wildernesses." Reading adds dimension and perspective to my understanding: sometimes contradicting, sometimes corroborating my observations, and sometimes answering questions that I have never even considered. For instance, a wood turtle stomps his feet and bangs his plastron against the soft earth to fool earthworms into thinking that it's raining; as the worms flee to the surface of the soil, escaping what they perceive as the imminent danger of drowning, the turtle eats them.

After perusing the stacks at the nearby Dartmouth College library, I spent the following day at home wading through *Turtles: Perspectives and Research,* a multiauthored, exhaustive volume that is to turtle literature what War and Peace is to Russian literature. The table of contents is divided into broad categories—taxonomy, evolution and zoo geography, methods of study, vital functions, sensory processes, reproduction and development, population dynamics: 602 pages of natural and unnatural turtle history. The bibliography alone is 65 pages, the index 27.

I went first to the index. Checking "painted," I was sent to *Chrysemys picta,* the turtle's pseudonym, where I uncovered eighty-three alphabetized topics, most with multiple page listings. One topic, "eggs," has fifteen separate listings.

From "a" to "w," "activity" to "water regulation," in scores of numerical references the painted turtle's dossier stretched before me like my uphill, washed-out driveway. Downshifting, I picked my way through the book, checking each of more than two hundred listings under *Chrysemys picta* .

Along the way, I was frequently surprised. In the name of behavioral science, for instance, several men have fashioned careers out of administering electric shocks to captive painted turtles and, as a result of their diligent Third Reich research, have concluded that, yes, you can teach old turtles new tricks. I learned that turtles have emotions; that they become aggressive when injected with male hormones. That their color preferences change with age: adults prefer blue and violet; young, red and yellow. And that they hyperventilate, known in turtle circles as "episodic breathing," beginning each series with an exhale, the opposite of human beings.

I also learned that basking painted turtles pump blood to their dark carapace to heat up and pump it away to cool down; that turtles swimming under ice absorb long wavelengths of light, raising their core temperature above that of the water; that for this species, it's easier to gain heat than to lose it; and that dead painted turtles heat up more slowly than live ones. One author believes that females pee on their nest sites to soften the soil before digging, to moisten the eggs, to kill bacteria, to repulse egg predators by offending their noses and taste buds, and to confuse avian predators by both compacting the soil after egg deposition and camouflaging the site. Not everyone is in agreement with this theory.

There was much more. For example, painted turtles orient by topographic and celestial clues. I learned that painted turtles are divided into four subspecies, or races, which range over most of the United States and southern Canada, with one race confined to Chihuahua, Mexico; that at 240 painted turtles per acre, a Michigan pond sponsors the highest known density of turtles.

After sitting for seven hours reading in my good-for-the-back, imported Swedish chair—the one without the backrest that tilts me forward onto padded knee supports—I learned that my back ached and that it was time to return to the lake.

Traveling across the interstate, traversing both the north- and southbound lanes of Interstate 91, is an achievement for a turtle, particularly an irascible thirty-pound snapping turtle whose sense of appropriate timing had to have been impaired: it was midafternoon on the first day of the July Fourth weekend.

Linny and I spotted the turtle as she entered the ranks of grass next to the shoulder along the southbound way. We stopped the car and realized that her westward progress would be impeded by a picket fence beyond the tall grass in front of her. We retrieved the turtle, fearing that a return trip across the interstate would prove fatal. I picked her up by her long spiny tail, held her at arms length (the only safe way to transport a snapper), and placed her on the floor of the front seat of our car.

Off we went to the grocery. The three of us. Linny drove and I minded the turtle, keeping the beast occupied and well away

45

from Linny's legs. Entertaining a snapping turtle is no easy task, particularly when your feet and the turtle's prehistoric head are squeezed into the same small space. Luckily for me, the turtle played ostrich, at least initially, hiding her head under the over-hanging console—a feature that makes an old Volvo wagon ideal for transporting an acrimonious chelonian.

During our brief stop at the grocery store, the snapper grew restless. Too dimwitted to appreciate being rescued, she backed up, forcing me out of the car and into the parking lot. Clapping her steel-trap jaws, she reached her long, thick neck out and over her upper shell, and held me at bay beside my own car, entrench-ing herself in the passenger space in the front seat. I saw her pink throat, the blood in her eyes, and knew there would be no reason-ing with this macabre Mesozoic throwback. I swore I'd never save another snapping turtle. The turtle, of course, ignored my rant-ing. A few pedestrians passed by, and with looks that suggested I should move to the cashew factory, watched me scream at a turtle as big as a serving tray. After coaxing her head back under the console, we drove home. I released the turtle in the front yard and watched in amazement as she struck the air with serpentine swiftness and directionless rage. Our dog learned quickly that the safest way to approach a snapping turtle is from the rear. Each time the dog advanced, the turtle rose on her broad hind legs, leaned forward so that her head hugged the ground, pivoted with unexpected speed, and thrust her neck nine inches beyond the edge of her carapace. Mouth agape, she struck with the speed of a rattlesnake. The dog maintained a safe distance.

Snapping turtles, *Chelydra serpentina*, are the largest fresh-water turtles in New England, and the most common and most widely distributed turtle in North America. The combined range of the four subspecies extends from the Rocky Mountains to the Atlantic seaboard and south from southern Canada all the way to

Ecuador. This enormous range, spanning nearly two-thirds of the United States, inevitably puts snapping turtles in close proximity to people. As is often the case with large, formidable creatures, we tend to endow them with attributes beyond reason.

When I was a boy, I met an old Long Island bayman who haunted the clam flats and salt marshes of the South Shore, and who claimed snapping turtles could bite broom handles in half. In fact they have been known to bite the legs off ducks; in the early days of Long Island duck farms, snappers feasted on the plump white ducklings, crippling and maiming thousands. Biting broom handles in half is modest stuff compared with the other exploits credited to snapping turtles. I found an old reference book that claimed that snapping turtles, after clamping their jaws on their victims, are unwilling or unable to let go until sundown or until thunder rolls from the sky. A Lake Fairlee bass fisherman told me that when beheaded, a snapping turtle will keep its jaws fixed on its victim for six to eight hours or until night falls, whichever comes first.

Despite anecdotal evidence to the contrary, the turtle is ferocious only on land, when searching for a nest site, or when removed from the water. Even large turtles that have been fighting fiercely on land become quiescent when placed in water and will attempt to swim away rather stand their ground. Summer bathers have nothing to fear from snapping turtles, which remain docile even if stepped on. Several summers ago, an aquatic biology class visited the shallow marshes on the north end of Lake Fairlee, and the students teetered across a series of small boulders. After six people had crossed, the fourth boulder moved away.

The submissive reaction of a submerged snapping turtle toward people, however, does not extend toward other animals. Snappers are voracious predators and scavengers, and consume legions of aquatic creatures, mostly fish and frogs. Occasionally, they pull waterfowl down from below. In the summer of 1977, a snapping turtle killed and ate two loon chicks on Conway Lake in northeastern New Hampshire. Young muskrats, water shrews, star-nosed moles, garter snakes, and aquatic insects, large and small, round out the snapping turtle's diet.

Hal Borland's entry for July 6 in *Book of Days* describes a struggle between a five-foot water snake and a snapping turtle:

> When I first saw them the snake was in those wire-cutter jaws, only the front two-thirds of its body free.
>
> It was a hopeless fight. . . . The snake hammered at the snapper's head and neck, striking repeatedly with no effect. It threw a coil of its body around the snapper's shell, tightened till its muscles corded, and the snapper merely braced its feet. With a twist, the snake flipped the turtle onto its back. The turtle's hind feet reached and raked with vicious claws and the snake's hold loosened. The turtle scrambled to its feet again.
>
> Half a dozen times the snake looped and squeezed, with no effect at all. The turtle kept shifting its hold, each new bite taking more of the snake's vitality. Finally the snake swung a body coil toward the turtle's neck, its one last chance for victory. Had it been able to catch the neck, the battle would have been over, probably a Pyrrhic victory, for the snake was crucially hurt. But it failed. The turtle, snapping with amazing speed, caught the snake just behind the head. That settled it, though the snake flipped the turtle over twice more in its desperate thrashing. At last it began to relax, the relaxation of defeat and death.

Our turtle was looking for sandy soil for her nest when Linny and I found her on the interstate. The warmer the weather the faster her embryos would develop. During the most favorable conditions, the average clutch of snapping turtle eggs laid in Lake Fairlee's sand requires between twelve and sixteen weeks to hatch.

Near lakes and ponds where summer people have extirpated the skunks, turtle eggs enjoy an almost predation-free incubation.

But newly hatched snapping turtles are vulnerable to herons, bit-terns, crows, gulls, otters, and raccoons which enjoy dining on the half-dollar-sized hatchlings. And on more than one occasion, I have examined bullfrog stomachs crammed with tiny turtles.

People have been eating snapping turtles for centuries, con-cocting a thick, rich soup—black as marsh mud—from the bulging limb muscles. I have found several commercial brands on grocers' shelves in the Midwest, and Philadelphia claims to be the capital of the U.S. turtle soup market.

I found another use for snapping turtles in an obscure text written by the late Carl Schmidt, a noted herpetologist with the Philadelphia Academy of Sciences. During a comprehensive study of the habits of these turtles, Schmidt discovered an elderly man who employed a tethered snapping turtle to locate drowned bod-ies in weedy southern swamps. If that turtle was anything like our turtle, a poor bloated fellow on the bottom of some dismal swamp would be better off lost.

After two days at our house, which included starring in a one-minute "nature spot" for the local television station that took most of an afternoon to film, the turtle had had enough. When-ever she heard my footfalls, she rose and snapped. She had a mis-sion to complete. We had human house guests, as well: my cousin Norman, a violinist with sensitive fingers and a sense of humor, along with his squeamish friend Phoebe. We arranged the car for the trip to Lake Fairlee, Norman and I in the front, Phoebe and the turtle squeezed in back. Imprisoned in a large cardboard box that was jammed against the hatchback with its flaps closed flat, the snapper seemed introspective and did not move.

For the length of our driveway, all went well. Then, the turtle awoke. I saw her in the rearview mirror—hatchet faced, beady eyed. She pried open the box, and began hauling herself over the top. I sounded the tocsin, and, just as the turtle left the box, Phoebe left the back seat. She leapt in front between Norman and the gear shift. I swerved down Bloodbrook Road, one hand on the wheel, one hand fending off the turtle with the box, amid hysterical laughter and wild chelonian hissing.

Arriving at Lake Fairlee, we released the turtle into the marsh. She rattled the cattails, heading for deeper water. Submerged, she pushed through stems of white waterlilies and pink smartweed, pulling flowers below the surface. As bouquets of waterweeds sank and rose, sank and rose, I wondered how soon the turtle would leave the water to dig her nest and how many of her hatchlings would survive the trek across Route 244 to enter the marsh at the mouth of Blood Brook.

The Alpine
Tundra Frontier

I spend June days on the summit of Mount Washington, and find
vestiges of the arctic: dwarf flowers scattered in the barrens like
chips fallen from a rainbow, and the secret embossments of lichen
on rock. I come for meltwater streams and wild weather, to get a
sense of what Blood Brook valley may have been like eleven thousand years ago, after the glaciers withdrew, leaving tundra and
boulder fields across New England.

Near the tollhouse at the base of the Mount Washington
Auto Road, a humming wind held black flies at bay—always a relief—and swayed the tender new leaves of sugar maple and American beech. I wore a dark sleeveless shirt, luxuriating in the sun
like an Arizona lizard. What looked like a benign cloud bonnet
covered the mountain. From the base elevation of only 1563 feet,
wrapped in mid-June warmth, I could neither see nor feel the
wind that assaulted the summit at sixty miles per hour, with
gusts over eighty. The New Hampshire Parks Department, afraid

that flailing car doors would crush fingers and arms or dent other parked cars, had closed the Auto Road to all but essential vehicles. Fortunately, they viewed my assignment to write an essay for Yankee as essential and let my family pass with a warning.

Driving to the 6288-foot summit was like traveling north from central New Hampshire or Vermont to the Quebec tundra and also like going back in time. Every thousand feet we climbed was the ecological equivalent of moving several hundred miles farther north or retreating several thousand years into the past. The familiar green woods of maple and beech yielded to evergreens, which started off straight and tall in the ravine forest at 2500 feet and then collapsed at 4800 feet into a gnarled, twisted mat, called krummholz, or crooked wood. Red spruce and balsam fir made up the conifer forest at lower elevations, but black spruce replaced red spruce in the krummholz and extended to treeline at 5200 feet, rarely raising a branch more than twelve inches above the ground. This miniaturization was dictated by climate, not age, for these four- or five-inch trees may be more than a hundred years old. Beyond treeline, ragged patches of krummholz cowered in the lee of boulders or wherever snow accumulates, sheltered from frigid, furious, branch-pruning winds and sand-blasting ice crystals. Blood Brook, 9000 B.C.

A thousand feet below the summit, near mile marker 7 on the Auto Road, lay a flat, rock-strewn piece of land called the Cow Pasture, gateway to the Alpine Garden. I reached the pasture, turned the car off, and listened to the wind roaring in tongues. Because of his limited formal training in meteorology, Casey, then two years old, didn't hear wind; he heard lawn mowers and chain saws, and insisted on seeing them.

I put on four layers of clothing, pulled down my wool cap, and opened the door. Before my foot settled on the ground, my cap took off. In sixty-mile-an-hour wind, it flew like a dunlin. As my coat inflated around me, I gave chase, leaping, lunging, lean-ing over frost-fractured rocks, almost airborne myself. By the time I reached the first cairn that marked the steep trail into the Alpine Garden, less than two hundred yards from the car, my hat had probably settled into the town of North Conway, ten miles away.

I have visited Mount Washington on sweet days, rare, warm, windless mornings one never forgets: red sun rises above Wildcat Mountain, igniting a peach-colored sky, and ground fog creeps through the valley. On such a day you feel as if you can see for-ever. To the north, Lake Umbagog; to the south, Lake Winnepe-saukee: the kind of day that inspired P. T. Barnum to proclaim that the view from Mount Washington is "the second greatest show on earth." And when it's particularly clear, New York's Adirondack Mountains appear in the west, more than one hun-dred and twenty miles away. Although I have glimpsed the At-lantic Ocean in the east—a flicker at Harpswell Neck, Maine—I never have seen Boston's Prudential Building from the summit, which popular lore claims is possible.

Gentle weather, however, is rare. Usually, it's as grueling as the arctic. Sitting in the middle of several storm tracks, Mount Washington has recorded winds 100 miles per hour every month of the year. In June 1990 the winds averaged 25.4 miles per hour, with the highest recorded speed 90 miles per hour. On only two days in June 1988 did they average less than 15 miles per hour, and on another two days, gusts exceeded 100 miles per hour; 107 miles per hour was the month's high that year. In 1934 the wildest wind ever recorded outside of a tornado struck the sum-mit at 231 miles per hour.

Winds chill everything. The mean temperature for July 1990 was 49.3 degrees Fahrenheit, with a high of 63 degrees and a low of 32 degrees. At an average temperature of 48.7 degrees, July is the warmest month on the mountain.

To the wind and cold add clouds, which block the sun 75 percent of the time. Last July there was only one clear day. Alpine Garden plants, in fact, depend on cold fog as their principal source of moisture. One summer morning Linny awoke at Lake-of-the-Clouds Hut to find the Alpine Garden caked with three inches of rime ice. By 10:00 A.M. it had all melted.

The arctic-alpine zone is the most extensive (and the most fragile) biologic province in the world: stretching across the northern hemisphere from Greenland to Alaska, and from Siberia to Scandinavia, capping the mountain ranges of every continent above timberline, and crossing the barrens of Patagonia. The White Mountains' alpine zone is among the world's smallest. Nestled between Mount Eisenhower and Mount Madison in the Presidential Range, it covers slightly less than seven and a half square miles. Mount Washington's Alpine Garden forms the centerpiece of the region. Here, in the lee of the summit, 110 species of flowering plants occur. Two-thirds of these plant species are restricted to the alpine and arctic tundra; for most of them, New Hampshire is the southern end of their range.

Standing by the cairn, I looked across an austere, boulder-strewn landscape and imagined herds of musk-ox grazing on threads of Bigelow's sedge. On the advice of a friend, I once climbed Mount Jacques Cartier in Quebec's Chic Choc Mountains to see woodland caribou on alpine tundra, a scene that must have been common along Blood Brook after the retreat of the last glacier, and on Mount Washington only a few thousand years ago. I reached the summit of Cartier at 5:00 A.M., searched everywhere, and found no caribou. Several hours later, intensely disappointed, I scrambled onto the roof of a cabin and scanned the tundra north and west of Jacques Cartier. A lone caribou crossed the crest of the next mountain, walked down an apron of tundra, and disappeared into the elfin timber along the edge of a small lake. A water pipit sang. A golden eagle rose above horizon. Simultaneously and surprisingly, I realized that if I could sense Blood Brook's cool past in Quebec, I could sense its future in Virginia; for several decades Vermont winters have been warmer and shorter than usual, and southern birds such as turkey vultures, blue-gray gnatcatchers, red-bellied woodpeckers, and Carolina wrens have moved into the state. Time and distance are relative and inseparable, each a component of the other.

As a raven arrowed over, lofted by the wind, its shadow interrupted my reverie. A black wolf spider scurried from boulder to boulder, while another, toting a silk basket crammed with eggs, paused in the lee of my boot. Like my dark shirt, which was by then buried under layers of clothes, black spiders absorb heat, an advantage for a cold-blooded animal whose body temperature is at the mercy of its surroundings. Of the more than two thousand species of insects collected on the summit of Mount Washington, only ninety-five are native. The rest had blown up from the lower slopes to become spider fodder. The wind shanghais larger animals, too. I once flushed a wind-drifted woodcock from a patch of mountain avens. Bracing itself in the current, the woodcock rose above the Garden, banked like a billiard ball, and disappeared into an invisible deciduous pocket far below, all in a few milliseconds.

The clouds began to disperse, the sun peeked out, and the wind petered to a more comfortable twenty miles per hour. Before hiking into the Alpine Garden, I decided to check back with Linny and Casey, who had elected to picnic in the Cow Pasture, close to the car, just in case the world turned upside down.

Halfway down the trail, I saw the White Mountains appear in the south, rolling away, blue-gray in the haze. Ann Zwinger was right when she wrote that in an alpine meadow, "the only objects larger than small are boulders." Tens of centuries of freezing and thawing have pushed rocks to the surface everywhere. Across the level part of the Garden, I saw circles and polygons of rock. Soil squeezed up between them. On slight inclines the patterns change to stripes of rock, and, where the slope steepens, to garlands. At my feet, mats of tiny diapensia, white flowers with red-tinted green leaves, cushioned the ground. Its red blush caused by antho-cyanin, the same pigment that ignites October maples, converts incident sunlight to heat, and protects the plant against ultravio-let radiation, which can be extreme in thin alpine air. I stepped from rock to rock like a boy avoiding sidewalk cracks, for flowers filled all the spaces. Wands of Lapland rosebay, a bonsai rhodo-dendron with bell-shaped, magenta flowers, each a miniature replica of a lowland rhododendron, rose a few inches above pros-trate tangles of evergreen leaves. Near the rosebay, a tight, low weave of alpine azalea sparkled with a smattering of pink quar-ter-inch flowers.

Because the growing season is short—winter is never more than seventy-five days away—and the climate Draconian, Lapland rosebay, diapensia, and alpine azalea bloom early, as soon as the temperature rises above freezing. Though they grow at a normal rate, they add only a few evergreen leaves each year, and most new growth gets clipped by the elements. Scattered over the rocky, windswept plains where snow cover is thin and frost is deep, from Labrador to Alaska to Scandinavia, the compact mats of these plants baffle the wind. On warm days heat trapped in air spaces between their leaves forms a sanctuary for insects and spi-ders.

A ground beetle trundled out from under a diapensia, crossed a boulder, then disappeared into a weft of azalea branches.

Between the boulders, three species of dwarf willow had set seed, and a scattering of alpine bilberry and arctic bearberry unfurled tiny flowers like pieces of a torn quilt. A green swath of mountain avens, still several days from flowering, traced a stream across the garden like the alders that follow Middle Brook uphill from the Lake Fairlee. A white-throated sparrow whistled. A junco stuttered. Returning to the Cow Pasture, I left the trail and hopped the rocks again. I found several stands of alpine bluet, their petals bleached as white as birch bark, a patch of mountain heath with a few bell-shaped, pale purple flowers, more diapensia and Lapland rosebay, and a shrew. But I never found my hat.

Beyond the Green Lawn

I hate to mow the lawn. It's a wearisome chore, performed under the weight of the summer sun. When the dew lifts from Blood Brook valley, which can be as late as noon, I set my course and begin. The blade slices and the vent spits pieces of green, green, green—timothy and Kentucky bluegrass—then a spray of purple, red, and yellow as vetch and hawkweed bow to the mower. What I cut are three thousand square feet of pedigreed grasses, carefully bred and randomly planted, which secures our view, enhances our house, and (the upkeep of which) tires my back. A monotonous and seemingly endless wave of grass stretches ahead of me, beyond the stone wall and across my neighbor's meadow.

In Vermont most grasslands are pastures and meadows, ephemeral plant communities that depend on people to survive. Without mowers or livestock they would slowly choke. If I didn't cut our meadow in autumn, the following spring a transition community crowded with perennials, goldenrods, milkweeds, asters, fleabanes, cinquefoils, and clovers would flourish, eventually giving way to sun-loving shrubs, blackberry, raspberry, and black raspberry, whose seeds are dispersed by birds. Next would come gray birch, pin cherry and fire cherry, white pine, and aspen, which, in turn, would yield to shade-tolerant trees like sugar maple, beech, and hemlock.

As I follow the mower around the house, I see immigrants of the immense interior grasslands which have been brought by settlement to the East's manmade, lilliputian prairies. Black-eyed Susans and blue-eyed grasses, both prairie wildflowers, grew more abundant and spread eastward as the forests of Indiana, Ohio, Pennsylvania, and New York fell before the long-handled ax. A century ago, when Blood Brook's meadows extended over Spaulding Hill and Bald Top, prairie birds like vespers and grasshopper sparrows raised their voices above the summer flowers; eastern meadowlarks whistled from nearby trees and stone walls, and the bubbling song of bobolinks filled the valley. Bobolinks still frequent the larger, uncut meadows, raining their song on acres of golden Alexanders, but I have never seen vesper and grasshopper sparrows or meadowlarks in the valley. Although Blood Brook's meadows are just a remnant of that nineteenth-century agrarian age, when 75 percent of Vermont's forests was cleared for grazing, the gates to the vast Midwest prairies are still ajar.

I mow several times a summer, just enough to stem the rising tide of seedling willows and aspens. These drift in as seeds from the edge of the woods or sprout as suckers from parent plants whose roots tunnel through the earth. Abundant moisture encourages shrubs and trees, which are inhibited by severe drought, to succeed grass. Although it takes me two hours to mow the lawn, I now know it could be much worse. If I had to mow the original North American prairie, more than one million square miles of grass, it would take me about nine million years working eight hours a day. If I volunteered to also take care of the desert grasslands of the Southwest, the Palouse prairie of southeastern Washington, and the interior grasslands of California, all isolated mature grasslands, I would be busy for another million years. Fortunately, other arrangements were made for maintaining the grasslands: drought.

Pausing for a moment, I examine timothy, three feet tall and heavy with pollen. I squeeze the hollow stem, running my fingers upward to the first joint. At each joint, the base of a leaf wraps around the stem, forming a sheath; extending up from its base, the long, narrow leaf tapers to a point. Leaves alternate up the stem, one to a joint. The timothy stem ends in a compact, cylindrical cluster of tiny odorless flowers without petals and sepals. No frills are needed to attract insects, for the pollen of grass flowers is posted by the wind. Yellow pollen dusts my hand.

The origin of timothy is obscure. Some botanists believe it was a native eastern North American grass that was sent to Europe and widely used as livestock feed. When timothy subsequently returned to America, naturalists mistook it for a European native. Other accounts claim that this grass, grown in European soil since the Stone Age, came to America with the colonists, who cultivated it for their horses and then scattered it from pasture to pasture and along roadsides all the way to the Pacific Coast. Mingling on my lawn with timothy is Kentucky bluegrass, velvet grass, and foxtail barley. Both the bluegrass and the velvet grass were definitely imports from Europe which dispersed beyond the cleared Northeast. Foxtail barley, a native of the western prairie, then moved east as the deciduous woods were cleared.

The characteristics of grasses which allow them to tolerate mowing have allowed them to survive drought and fire and a galaxy of grazers, from prehistoric horses and mammoths to grasshoppers and meadow voles. The biomass of grass is mostly below the ground. Roots and rhizomes, those creeping, underground stems that send grass sideways into Linny's garden no matter how many times we yank up the shoots, account for more than 60 percent of the weight of big bluestem, a grass so tall it can hide a person. If placed end to end, the grass roots in a square yard of prairie soil four inches deep might run for up to twenty miles, and are so fused and intertwined that a hundred years ago farmers had to break the prairie with oxen and steel blades before they could plow it.

In Kansas I saw the leaves of Canada wild rye and Indian grass rolled into tubes to reduce the surface area they exposed to the arid wind. In South Dakota, mats of brown buffalo grass and shriveled blue grama curled close to the ground. After rain, all four species began to uncurl. In most varieties of flowering plants, meristems, the growing tissue that produces new stems, leaves, and branches, occur at the tips of growing shoots. Meristems rise with the plant as it grows. In grass, the growth occurs at the base of the leaves and stems. New tissue thus pushes the older leaves and stems higher toward the summer sun. Mowing and grazing, which cut off the growing tips of most other plants—and drought and fire, which sear them—leave grass practically unharmed; the large meristem at the base of the plant, hidden by a protective blanket of soil, simply sends up new shoots.

Since most grasses contain silica (the abrasive ingredient in sand), which stiffens their long leaves, mammals that graze on grass need exceedingly tough teeth. From horses to meadow voles, grass eaters show similar dental patterns: high-crowned teeth with alternating folds of dentine and enamel, teeth resistant to erosion. Several years ago, I fingered fossil molars of a woolly mammoth and an American mastodon. The surface of the mammoth's shoebox-sized tooth, a series of parallel oval ridges of enamel separated by a narrow valley of cementum, looked like an aerial photograph of the Ohio River Indian mounds and felt like furrowed iron. Had the tooth been prone to decay it would have required an Ice Age dentist with a jackhammer to fill it. Yet grass gradually wore down these mammoth teeth, and the behemoths had to grow six sets of molars during their lifetime. *Mastodon* means nipple tooth: the surface of the mastodon's tooth looked like a field of drumlins, all cones and valleys, shaped to chew soft leaves and twigs, which are less apt to erode cusps than is silica-rich grass. Even dainty grasshoppers which cut grass have sharper, bulkier mandibles than those do those which cut forbs. It's like comparing wire cutters to scissors.

After Vinny, my neighbor's itinerant cow, crops a mouthful of our fibrous lawn, her lower jaw slides sidewise. Her teeth grind grass and green juice and bubbles seep from the corners of her mouth, staining her lips. She needs a very specialized stomach and intestines to digest her favorite food. Only microbes can digest cellulose, the principal component of plant cell walls. Vinny swallows grass, lets it ferment in the first chamber of her four-chambered stomach, and then spits up the cud, chews it, and reprocesses it in the other three chambers. Despite all this processing and reprocessing, I still recognize some undigested grass blades in Vinny's manure piles, which she deposits on the driveway.

Some of my neighbors torch their fields in spring to remove old growth and to stop plant succession. In this way, they do for their meadows what nature does for the prairie. Fire destroys last year's brown withered stalks and warms the earth, encouraging the growth of new shoots while scorching invading trees and shrubs. When I burn a brush pile, I burn it in the meadow in the middle of a patch of willows so that the heat will sear the shrubs while it consumes the brush. Within a few days, green grass pokes through a coat of ashes.

Western grasslands are prone to fire; it's part of their cycle. By autumn, grass stems and leaves stand brown and dry, and are extremely combustible; roots and rhizomes live on underground, insulated below the soil. Following a rainfall gradient from east to west, plant geographers divide the prairies into three broad communities named according to the height of the dominant grasses. In the east, tallgrass. In the west, shortgrass. Mixed grass, a wide band whose boundary moves west with excessive rain and east with drought, is a broad transition zone between the two. All three prairie types burn, but they burn differently.

When I was a graduate student, my fire ecology class burned a range of shortgrass—the grassland in the rain shadow of the Rockies, which extends east across Montana to western North Dakota, and south through the Llano Estacado, or Staked Plains of west Texas. This shortgrass fire, fed by scanty fuel, did not produce a lot of heat. A horned lizard flattened out as the fire passed over its back, then got up and crawled away. A jackrabbit bounded ahead of the flames, moving at a more leisurely pace than if it had been chased by a coyote. Just for the record, I jumped a line of fire.

Several years ago, I saw lightning spark a mixed-grass prairie in Wind Cave National Park. Safely seated in my car, I was watching a thunderhead build above a busy village of black-tailed prairie dogs when the sky suddenly ripped open, and three white, flickering shafts like electric harpoons drove straight down to earth, striking behind a knoll about half a mile from where I was parked. The prairie dogs never stopped feeding, barking, or kissing. Twenty minutes later, after the storm had passed south toward Nebraska, tendrils of smoke rose into the evening sky as fire purified one acre of mixed-grass prairie before the Park Service arrived and extinguished the flames.

Tallgrass prairie, richest in fuel, burns the brightest and hottest. Its deep, black soil, watered by up to forty inches of rain a year, once ran from northwestern Indiana to east Texas and north into Manitoba. Indian and lightning fires stopped the forest from advancing along the prairie's eastern front and restricted gallery forests to river valleys. Fueled by tall, sun-cured grass and fanned by the wind, fierce tallgrass fires were stopped only by rivers and by rain. Now it is standard policy to control or put all fires out. Driving west on Interstate 70 through the Flint Hills of northeastern Kansas, I saw dark green forests covering what had once been tallgrass prairie.

As much as I dislike mowing, burning my lawn is not a consideration. My house, pine with cedar shingles, is crisp and dry, sits in the middle of the lawn, and would flare in a second. There are safer, less tiring ways to keep the grass short. Linny suggests sheep or goats, maybe a dairy cow. I prefer bison, but with only three thousand square feet of grass, my yard would soon be pulverized by their busy, cloven hooves.

My lawn is even too small for a 100-pound pronghorn, but it does support a legion of grasshoppers, particularly Carolina locusts that rise from the grass like popcorn from a hot skillet as I push the mower forward. Actually, grasshoppers consume more grass than all other above-ground grazers combined. Only root-hungry nematodes—microscopic roundworms, whose populations number in the millions per square foot—eat more grass. The more extensive the grassland, the greater the variety of grasshoppers found there. Kansas entertains over three hundred species, more than six times as many as Vermont, and no state in the prairie region has fewer than a hundred.

I stop mowing, turn my binoculars around, and look through the wide magnifying end at the busy, carefree world of grasshoppers. They slice through the greenery with sharp, sliding mandibles that move from side to side, the left always overlapping the right, dropping as much as they eat. I grab a grasshopper and hold him firmly in my hand as he scratches my palm with spiked feet. "Tobacco juice" dribbles from his mouth, staining my fingers an inky brown. He kicks and scrapes and twists in my hand, a corkscrew in a shell. I place him on the ground, and he flies a short distance until satisfied he is no longer in danger, then he climbs back up some timothy and resumes feeding.

Although I have never visited a prairie in late summer, I imagine the noise of the insects is deafening, for in August my lawn and meadow reverberate with the sounds of grasshoppers, crickets, and katydids. Nowhere along Blood Brook is the chorus louder than in the meadows. Grasshoppers and katydids live out the length of their lives under the high suns of a single season. Last year's eggs hatch when the meadow grows warm, each wingless nymph already a miniature replica of its parents. The young grow in size and develop wings as the grasses ripen: when the maple blushes, they scrape and scratch their wings until silenced by frost.

My late summer mowing does more than just displace hungry Carolina locusts: I also disrupt their mating rituals. Two or three feet above the lawn, male grasshoppers hover on broad black wings edged with yellow along the rear. Their vibrating wings make a slow buzzing sound that attracts females and other males who compete for the attention of the gravid females. Whenever a female grasshopper lands, three or four males move toward her. If I get too close, they snap into the air, then reassemble wherever the female lands.

Cricket music is an unequivocal sign of September. A few field crickets always move from the meadow into our living room whenever a cold front rolls out of the north. They scurry along the walls, hidden by furniture, traveling from one throw rug to another. From dusk to dawn territorial males send out salvos of triple chirps or continuous, high-pitched trills to attract free-ranging female crickets to their corner of the house. Going to bed is like going camping, as we drop off to sleep lulled by indoor cricket serenades.

Occasionally a cricket crosses open ground, slipping in full view over the tile floor. When Casey was a toddler, he would spot one, drop to all fours, and trail it with short-lived but acute determination. Usually, the cricket got away or Casey's attention waned, but once in a while he would grab it and beam. Because I wanted to encourage his interest in small forces of nature, those seemingly prosaic beings that most of us long ago ceased to consider, I would tell him about crickets.

I would tell him that crickets are among the oldest insects, that their ancestors—the planet's first minstrels—fiddled to the Tyrannosaurus, and that their music is mechanical, not vocal. The base of each wing has a file and a scraper, I would tell him, and a vibrating membrane, the tympanum; the file of each wing rubs against the scraper of the other wing, setting both tympana in motion, filling the house with prairie music. I would conclude by telling him that crickets hear through the middle section of their front legs, the tibia.

Unimpressed with my pedantry, Casey would eye a black cricket scooting across the floor, and I'd try a less scholarly approach: "Let's get the cricket!" He would chase the cricket into a corner, scrambling across the tile floor like a splay-legged puppy. If it darted behind a bookcase, I would grab a yardstick and position Casey at one end of the bookcase, then attempt to push the cricket toward him from the other end. Responding to deep-seated instincts that have been buttressed through millions of generations, the cricket always stopped just short of Casey's outstretched arm.

If another cricket sang from a remote corner of the kitchen, Casey would crawl for it, the yardstick clutched in his fingers, clapping the floor. If I reached his quarry first, I would gently pick it up and let its song pour through my fingers—a metronome that keeps cadence with the changing season. Then I would place the cricket on Casey's knee. I believe it is important for him to touch living things, to touch the wildness of his backyard. If his overeager fingers crush the insect, so be it. A crushed field cricket is a small price to pay for broadening a little boy's landscape.

Continuing to mow, I cross the opening of a small burrow in the front yard, probably a chipmunk's. Without trees for shelter, many grassland mammals and reptiles (and even some birds) have become adept at burrowing. Rodents asleep in their burrows have little to fear except weasels and snakes, both of which prowl below the ground. One afternoon I watched a seven-foot bull snake emerge into the California sun, its sides swollen with ground squirrels. I counted four separate bulges—an entire family, I suspected.

Burrows also provide a constant temperature that protects the inhabitants from fire and from weather, which on the western grasslands can swing from broiling to frigid. In Vermont, near the unnamed fork of the East Branch of the Ompompanoosuc, I've seen eastern coyotes and red foxes dig whelping dens in the sandy meadows, and one June I watched woodchucks sunning themselves on a stone wall in the corner of a neighbor's pasture. In April, when the pasture grass first greened, the mother woodchuck exchanged her winter den in the woods for a hole under the rocks. There, in a burrow beneath the wall, she gave birth. As the sun rose, the rocks heated up. Such a burrow was the perfect place for a woodchuck family. The soil was brown and rich, just sandy enough so that rain would drain and not flood the sleeping chambers. The stone wall was a fortress; the pasture a larder. Behind the wall, a screen of thorny blackberries provided midday shade and caught the dust from Bloodbrook Road. The wood-chuck is one animal that has profited from the clearing of the Northeast.

For the past two years I have watched her raise a family in the boulders. A grizzly male, living across the pasture in a more traditional woodchuck setting—a mound of earth at the entrance to a main tunnel, tall grass and clover all around—visited the boulders each year in late April. He stayed two or three days, courting and sowing seed, then returned to the greening pasture. Thirty-two days later, the mother woodchuck whelped a litter of blind, naked pups.

The pups grew, nourished by rich milk. In late June, they assembled on the rocks to nurse and to eat sprigs of clover and alfalfa that their mother brought for them. A week later, they romped in front of the boulders, clipped nearby grass, and watched their mother graze in the pasture. When nearly six weeks old, the pups regularly rested on the stone wall, soaking up sun. When hungry, they cut their own greens in front of the wall or foraged on clover in the middle of the pasture. I watched the mother lead her troop single file along the wall and into the field. She rose on her haunches to scout for danger. The pup train kept moving, bumped into her, and derailed. No danger. The march resumed. Eventually, they reached the clover patch and feasted, chewing their way through ranks of perennials. If I wandered too close to the rocks, she would sit up and whistle, and the pups would vanish into their den. It was an idyllic life: they had few predators, and their closest human neighbors, who were not inclined to garden, tossed them bits of celery and apple. The mother only had one litter a year, for no matter how perfect a woodchuck's home, the growing season in Vermont is short. By August a woodchuck's efforts are entirely directed toward fattening up for winter.

When I was an undergraduate in Indiana, I had to memorize the scientific nomenclature for all forty-something species of mammals in that state. Of all the Latin nouns shoehorned into my consciousness, the woodchuck's name, *Marmota monax*, best recalls that night before the mammalogy final, when I sat transfixed on Latin terms delirious and surrounded by a halo of coffee and NoDoz. Marmota means marmot or mountain mouse. Monax means digger. Both epithets fit, for the woodchuck (or groundhog) digs compulsively in meadows and tallgrass prairies, and is therefore assigned to the same genus as marmots, whose homes are in the mountains.

Sometime during that long-ago night, I realized that the riddle, "How much wood . . . ?," could be restated in partial Latin: "How much marmota could a marmota monax monax if a marmota monax could monax marmota?" Now, whenever I think of a woodchuck the riddle surfaces like an old and now meaningless baseball statistic. I am left with the image of a family of plump grassland rodents grazing on a Vermont meadow, neither looking for their shadows in February nor forecasting the weather (which in New England is arbitrary and capricious), nor monaxing marmota.

If I didn't mow the lawn a couple of times a month, new species of wildflowers would bloom every week. Wild strawberry and downy blue violet, short plants with accelerated life cycles, flower and fruit before tall grass and clover close out the sun. In the meadow, Kentucky bluegrass blooms early for the same reason. Summer wildflowers keep pace with the rising canopy of grass. The taller flowers such as buttercup, orange hawkweed, yellow hawkweed, and fleabane bloom later; and the tallest flowers such as Canada goldenrod, New England aster, and milkweed bloom near the very end of a compact, concise Vermont summer.

Whenever I stop mowing to uproot a small aspen or willow, a

long, skinny root breaks the surface and leads me to another, until I unravel a genealogical puzzle. Each sapling is a shoot from a neighboring one, perhaps one uprooted some time ago. Pulling up seedling white pines is easier: one yank and it's gone; no sibling connections. I am glad I don't have to weed the prairies. Like a ship's anchor, purple prairie clover drives a taproot six feet through the sod, spreading most of its branches at the lower end of the root to avoid direct competition with the network of tallgrass roots that crowd the upper level of the soil. Knee-high purple coneflowers have eight-foot unbranched taproots, and compass plants prospect for water and nutrients straight down fourteen feet.

Lacking silica, some wildflowers discourage herbivores with chemical warfare. The bitter juice of milkweed is a good example. Stinging nettle and thistle have their spines. My neighbor's cattle avoid eating thistle, and in August his pasture is speckled with tall, prickly bouquets of lavender flowers. While uprooting nettle last summer, I tossed a plant behind me that struck Casey in the face. He cried for fifteen minutes!

Almost every month of the summer and fall, the meadow engages in a wild roulette of seed dispersal. Besides the wind, there are other seed dispersal strategies for meadow plants. Pin cherry and chokecherry hitch their fates to wayfaring birds, swapping a nutritious fruit for a free ride in a bird's digestive tract, and sprout where the meadow grades into lawn. Burrs and asters hitch free rides on my sweaters and socks. In both methods of seed dispersal, inner and outer animal transport, there is the element of chance: birds must relieve themselves, mammals must groom themselves in specific locations for successful germination.

Of all the strategies of meadow plant seed dispersal, relying on wind is the least trustworthy. To hedge its bets on landing in a suitable growing site, a single milkweed with five or six pods produces over one thousand seeds—about one hundred and eighty-five seeds per pod. As the pod ripens, it splits vertically, seam away from the stalk. Then, from top to bottom, the lips of the seam begin to roll back. The seeds, bound in a tight spiral, loosen.

The anatomy of the milkweed pod is a provident design, a lesson in solid geometry, for its shape allows for the most efficient use of space while placing the seed in a position that is accessible to the wind. A thin silk ribbon connects each seed to a pleated membrane that runs the length of the pod. The seeds curl around the membrane, overlapping each other so that the upper seeds, those adjacent to the open seam, are the first to meet the full force of the wind as the pod splits and curls back. After a seed leaves the pod, the one immediately behind it extends the length of its parachute and waits for the wind to snap its connective ribbon. The lining of the pod is smooth so that the seeds and their wispy parachutes slip easily into the wind. One by one the seeds are borne off.

Cowbirds fly up from the meadow at the sight of the mower. Their practice of brood parasitism—laying their eggs in the nests of other birds, which then incubate the eggs and fledge the chicks, often at the expense of their own young—freed them to follow the wandering herds of bison, which stirred up insects and seeds for them to eat. So closely tied were the two species that Plains Indians knew them as buffalo birds.

I saw cowbirds milling around bison in the mixed-grass prairies of South Dakota. I see them milling around cows at home in Blood Brook valley. They're in my yard, across the meadow, and in the pasture, little vagabonds that watch me push my mower across the lawn with the attention they once lavished on the hulking bison. Here they come to follow my mechanical, Sunday morning roar. My mower's spinning blades stir up grasshoppers and seeds, while keeping the woods at bay.

Flowers in the Wild

In Vermont spring comes slowly, as though from a long way off. I hear it in the two-note song of the chickadee which begins in mid-February while a still cold sun climbs noticeably higher in the sky. This is followed by the return of red-winged blackbirds, red-tailed hawks, and bluebirds, and the nesting of great horned owls. In early March, my neighbors begin to boil sap, the Connecticut River usually unlocks, skunks and raccoons awaken, and red-shouldered hawks arrive from the south. Lake Fairlee opens by mid-April. Peepers, wood frogs, and spotted salamanders spawn under April showers, while Blood Brook purls with meltwater. Full of promise, the valley prepares for another spring.

By late April, buds swell, tubers and corms sprout. Looking east to Bald Top, I see wisps of spring color tight against the twigs and branches: light gray of big-toothed aspen and yellow-green of quaking aspen, the copper-red of sugar maple; flat and somber green of pine and spruce; still gray, the leafless white ash and but-ternut.

And on the forest floor, puddles of wildflowers.

Many of the earliest, showiest spring wildflowers along Blood Brook are perennials with compressed life cycles which sprout, leaf, bloom, go to seed, and die back in less than six weeks. Every April they flash before me like a reverie. Bloodroot flourishes on the banks of an unnamed feeder stream that runs off Bald Top, then quickly fades. Bloodroot needs direct sunlight to grow, as well as a bed of moist soil, soil enriched by years of woodland growth. To that end, it flowers in late April before the hardwoods have leafed out. By mid-June, bloodroot has contributed its own leaves, stems, and white, oblong petals to the forest mulch. Spring ephemerals not only thrive in the valley, they serve its other lives. Carpetlike patches of trout lily temporarily lock up phosphorous, a valuable soil nutrient that might otherwise be washed into Blood Brook by the runoff from spring rain. When trout lily dies back and decomposes at the end of its short life cycle, a vernal dam of phosphorous is released back to the woodland.

Late last April, I found Dutchman's breeches, another spring ephemeral, flowering at the foot of a large sugar maple not far from the driveway. There was only a single delicate plant, with soft green leaves, deeply cut like fern fronds, below a leafless wand with six upside-down flowers. I fingered one of the four-petaled blossoms, no more than a half-inch across and three-quar-ters of an inch long, cream-colored with bright yellow tips. The genus name *Dicentra* means "two spurs," a reference to the two outer lobed petals that suggest inflated pantaloons hanging ankle-up on a clothesline. Dutchman's breeches is a powerful love charm for the Menominee of the western Great Lakes, and a vi-sual spring tonic to all those who know it. While I stood there, a bumblebee forced her way past the protective yellow lips, the belt of the breeches, and reached deep inside the spurs with her long proboscis to harvest the fragrant nectar without damaging the flower. Because of their short proboscises, honeybees cannot reach the spurs; I've watched a honeybee collect grains of pollen with her feet near the flower's mouth. Two of the flowers had holes in the ankles and were brown along the edges and opening into the nectaries, where a rapacious beetle had chewed into the spurs and stolen nectar without spreading pollen, foiling Dutchman's pollination strategy and bankrupting the flower.

For a long time I paid violets little attention. Because my mother had landscaped her Long Island flower beds with pansies, a cultivated violet with large, colorful blossoms, and because wild violets sprout in my lawn, I categorized them in my personal taxonomy as pedestrians, a category in which I included tulips, daffodils, and heal-all. I neither photographed nor wrote about violets. Yet the loss was mine.

Near the height of land on Spaulding Hill, the hardwood forest floor gently slopes toward the southeast; the soil is rich in humus and sponsors a cavalcade of wildflowers that open to the spring sun: round-lobed hepatica, bellwort, trout lily, Carolina spring beauty, and what I thought to be three species of violet: blue, white, and yellow. I used to walk through the spring woods and photograph hepatica and spring beauty, merely noting the violets.

I found that after hepatica, trout lily, and spring beauty had faded, violets still flowered. Nestling down to photograph a pale, lilac-colored northern blue violet, I pressed into the leaf litter. A bumblebee landed on the lower petal of a neighboring violet. She followed the nectar guides, which are directional color-lines on the petals, toward the flower's cream-colored center and then turned upside down, clutching the top petal as she worked the nectar spur that extended from the rear of the lower petal. The bee left dusted with pollen.

Prompted by the bee, I examined a violet and found five tiny green sepals, leaflike structures that enclose developing flowers, bent backward around the nectar sac. The curved sepals ensure that nectar-hungry insects will enter the front of the flower, brushing by the pollen on their way. Without this protection, beetles could chew their way in through the pollenless back door, sipping the nectar without doing their share of pollen scattering in return, just as they do with Dutchman's breeches.

When I returned home, I mentioned the violet and the bumblebee to Linny, who told me that ants and violets have complicated relationships, too. Ants collect violet seeds, bury them in their tunnels, and later eat the elaiosome, a small oil-rich projection on the seedcoat. While eating the elaiosome, ants scrape the seedcoat with their mandibles, which stimulates the seed to germinate. Since ants abandon their burrows every four or five weeks, seed buildup in an ant nest is not large, reducing competition among the germinating violets.

I went to Dartmouth's biology library to find out more. Violets, I read, are not the only flowers with ant-dispersed seeds: hepatica, bloodroot, wild ginger, Dutchman's breeches, and squirrel corn—all delicate spring ephemerals that tint Spaulding Hill—produce elaiosomes on their seedcoats which attract foraging ants. In addition, plants from seeds germinated in ant nests grow larger and more numerously than those randomly scattered by the parent plant.

I apologized to the violets, and thanked them for reminding me that "common" and "understood" are not synonymous. In every small ant mound in the lawn I learned to see the potential for flowers.

A week after I paid my dues to the violets, I found a Jack-in-the-pulpit in full flower near the base of a small sugar maple, just above a profusion of fiddleheads. Spaulding Hill was jubilant with birdsong: a black-and-white warbler; a tanager, singing like a hoarse robin; wood thrushes and veerys; and the sibilant cry of a broad-winged hawk. A tessellation of light and dark formed and reformed across the forest floor as new leaves swayed in the wind. This was the forest of middle May, cool and wet, green and brown, pulsating with urgency.

Jack's canopied pulpit shaded its inflorescence from the maple-filtered sunlight. At this stage, Jack's three-part leaves were no bigger than the flower. If there are two leaves and they continue to grow, eventually rising above the flower, then the plant is a female, a Jill-in-the-pulpit; if there is a single leaf, not much bigger than the flower, it is usually a male.

What makes the sex life of Jack-in-the-pulpit so intriguing is that this perennial wildflower has united in one body the characteristics of male and female. Unlike Hermaphroditus, however, Jack-in-the-pulpit reveals only one sex at time and can change sex from year to year. No stage in the sexual development of the flower is fixed, and as many as 50 percent of the plants on Spaulding Hill may switch sex each spring. This sex change, called sequential hermaphroditism, is determined by the amount of sugar converted and stored as starch over the course of the previous summer. By the end of the growing season, if a medium-sized Jack stores enough starch, it produces buds for two leaves and a female inflorescence, returning the following spring as a Jill. If, on the other hand, a female plant has a poor growing season, it returns as a Jack, with a smaller, single leaf and male floral parts. Plants without flowers are either young, sexless plants developing from seed or Jacks that have been emasculated by a poor growing season.

Only those Jacks with enough stored energy to produce large, fleshy red berries from the fertilized flower develop into females. Once the pollen grains have been collected by fungus gnats, the tiny male flowers of Jack-in-the-pulpit wither and die. Pollinated female flowers grow all summer. Because a plant with a single leaf could not support the growth of berries, sex change accompanies size.

I waited for fungus gnats to enter the pulpit under the arched canopy. Deceived by color and odor, the gnats mistook the Jack for the mushroom on which they mate and lay their eggs, and crawled down the spike to the pollen-bearing inflorescence. The hooded spathe, or modified leaf, shades the entrance, obscuring the opening through which the gnat entered the plant. Streaked with transparent lines, the side of the spathe allows tissue-filtered light into the flower. Eventually discovering they have been duped, gnats headed for the light, slid on the slippery walls of the spathe, dusting pollen over themselves, and eventually escaped through a tiny hole at the base of the flower where the spathe overlaps itself. I watched feeble-minded gnats leave one male flower and enter another. And another. Eventually, one gnat entered a Jill, whose spathe base overlaps so smoothly that it leaves no escape hole. The thrashing, incarcerated gnat pollinated the flower, then died at the base of the pulpit, deceived by the ministry, another lost soul.

To see a deciduous woodland orchid, a goddess among maple-woods wildflowers, I drive the back roads from West Fairlee to Sharon, winding across a mosaic of rich woods and meadow, eventually crossing the West Branch of the Ompompanoosuc River through a narrow covered bridge. A mile beyond Donner State Forest, a road forks to the right, runs uphill past a silver fox farm to a picture-perfect red farmhouse that sits at the head of a U-shaped glacial valley. Beyond the house, around and behind a hillock at the far end of the valley, a shady ravine hosts a large station of showy orchis, an uncommon woodland wildflower that I have not found on Spaulding Hill.

One spring more than a hundred plants bloomed in the moist soil. New sugar maple and beech leaves softened the sunlight, which spangled but did not heat the ground. The soil was rich and the compost deep. I touched one of the plants, studying its perfection. Two elliptical, four-inch leaves rose and spread from the base of a thick flower stalk that supported the five blossoms, each an inch long, which spiraled up from the middle of the stalk. Each flower had a soft mauve hood, formed by three sepals and two petals, which merged without fusing. The hood covered a long white lip that angled down from the stalk like an extended tongue. A single spur-shaped nectary hidden deep within the flower would supply sweets to an insect whose proboscis was long enough to reach the tube. Grooves in the lip would channel the proboscis toward the nectary, assuring a bumblebee or moth of a copious harvest and setting the stage for pollination.

As I backed away from the orchis, a huge bumblebee arrived, probably a queen. She probed for sweets, driving her long proboscis deep into the nectary and rupturing a thin membrane inside the flower so that an infertile stigma was forced downward, exposing two sticky pollen sacs, or pollinia.

One or both of these sticks to the bee's head and begins to dry. If a bee leaves the showy orchis before the sacs are firmly set, the pollinia stays with the flower. To encourage pollination, showy orchis has a hidden nectary, which requires a bee to break through the wall of nectary and to bore holes into the inner membrane. While a bee sips nectar from the intercellular spaces, the pollinia attaches to her head.

Nectar collected, the bee left, a single pollinium stuck to her head. Soon the membrane that supported that sac on the bee's head contracted, bending downward toward the tip of her proboscis at the precise angle needed to bring it in contact with the stigma of the next showy orchis that she visited. If the pollinium were to remain erect on her head, they would miss the stigma, failing to pollinate the next flower. After the bee left, the rostellum of the flower swung back into place so that the remaining sac remained damp and ready for the next potential pollinator.

With dusk gathering in the ravine and the bumblebee long gone, a white-lined sphinx moth arrived at an orchis. Iridescent wings quivering, belly bands shining, it hovered like a hummingbird with its tongue unfurled, sipping nectar. I could not see if pollinia had fixed on its head; it was too dark and the moth too fast.

My friend and former neighbor Sally Comstock called wildflowers by their country names: purple trillium was stinking Benjamin; trout lily was adder's tongue; marsh marigold was cowslip; bluets were Quaker ladies; joe-pye weed was queen-of-the-meadow. She spent her life on a Hartland knoll, facing the sun from the house she was born in. A fallen pine marked with the king's broad arrow lay in the woods behind the house. Sally and her sister Lucia married twins. Sally and Jack lived together for fifty-two years, raised three daughters and a son, ate dandelion and cowslip greens, and decorated sugar cookies with crushed butternuts. They grew big, sweet, juicy corn and melons which Sally sold from a table beneath maples her father had planted. As the produce ripened, the Comstocks played baseball games from a radio to scare away raccoons; on August nights I listened for the scores rising from her garden. Sally led me to Dutchman's breeches, showy orchis, and wild ginseng, which she dug from secret hollows between Windsor and Hartland. Sally scattered the crimson ginseng berries to aid germination before drying and selling the roots to Korean herbal dealers. When Sally died last August at eighty-three, the Presbyterian church overflowed with meadow flowers.

Sally prepared for spring. Every October, she potted a clump of hepatica that she had dug from the woods behind her house, and stored it in her basement, which she claimed was like being buried under snow. Having been down there, I believe her. Sometime in February—the actual date varied from year to year depending on Sally's mood—she would relocate the hepatica to a living room windowsill. A little water, a little sunlight, and by early March, the hepatica was in bloom, blue and lavender, sometimes white. In late April, Sally returned the plant to the woods. After so many Octobers, I imagine most of the hepatica that grew behind her house had cycled through her living room, some plants more than once.

Every species of wildflower is a composite of adaptations, including relationships with light, temperature, pollinators, soil organisms, and factors I cannot even guess at, all blended into colorful, often gorgeous arrangements of petals, sepals, stamens, and pistils. A complicated, intricate, very precise design—which people often see as a kind of decoration—is inseparable from both the beauty and the survival of a flower. Like Sally Comstock, wildflowers prepare for the future, enticing others to notice.

Birds Sowing
and Harvesting

Early last March, hundreds of silver maple buds lay frozen on the snow along a Connecticut River backwater not far from Lake Fairlee. Each swollen, copper-red bud had absorbed enough March sunlight to melt through the ice and seemed to lie in an icy crypt as much as two inches beneath the surface of the snow. Overhead, a silent red squirrel that had left the sheltered hemlocks and pines to feed in the windswept branches of the silver maples, licked the sweet drops of sap beading at the end of each severed twig.

The woods along Blood Brook are home to a great diversity of animal species, for with its layered vegetation—canopy, understory, shrub, herb, and soil surface—habitat and food are much more varied than in the meadow. Each tree provides a smorgasbord of leaves, stems, branches, buds, flowers, roots and rootlets, sap, bark, and seeds or fruit or nuts, that can be gnawed, chewed, bitten, nipped, swallowed, shredded, rolled, drained, perforated, peeled, masticated, and sucked dry by a legion of animals from mites to moose.

Important as a nurse tree that shelters seedling maples and as a source of wildlife food, the fast-growing, fast-spreading aspen that flanks our pond and invades the lawn has few rivals. Blood Brook beavers eat its inner bark and use the bare sticks to build dams and lodges. Moose browse the foliage, strip the bark, and chew the twigs. Ruffed grouse eat the buds in winter and, in spring, the catkins. Purple finches eat the buds, porcupine and meadow voles the bark, and snowshoe hare the twigs. Suckers vacuum up the seeds that settle to the bottom of Lake Fairlee. White-tailed deer rip off the leaves. Even red foxes sometimes chew the resinous buds.

Although white pine is less palatable than aspen, white-footed mice eat the seeds, then litter my office floor with the shells. In spring I find mourning dove and robin nests in the driveway pines, and during migration the pines host innumerable grackles and blackbirds that call attention to themselves with voluble, strident calls. I find that robins, wood thrushes, and chipping sparrows line their nests with white pine needles. Where pine has crowded out gray birch, closing the canopy and blocking the sunlight, the punky old birch stubs attract black-capped chickadees that excavate nest holes in the soft wood; where aspens have suffered the same the same fate, I find yellow-bellied sapsucker cavities. Wild turkey depend on stout-branched white pines for roosting trees. One winter afternoon I found a turkey killed by a fisher in a copse of big pine. Black and white wing feathers littered the snow.

On dry and windy winter days, winged hemlock seeds freckle the snow. Because the seeds absorb moisture, cone scales that enclose them open when dry and close when wet. Good seed crops occur every two or three years, a pattern that begins when the tree is thirty to fifty years old and that may continue for more than four hundred years; a pattern also indelibly etched in the genes of the northern finches—white-winged crossbills, red crossbills, pine grosbeaks, and purple finches—that travel from the Canadian hinterlands to Spaulding Hill during the bumper crop winters.

One September, three blue jays gathered green acorns from a neighbor's red oaks and planted them along the wooded edge of our meadow. Every bird disgorged a small pile of acorns, maybe four or five, then took each one a few feet away and pushed it into the soil, tucking it under leaf litter. Covering the acorns with leaves reduces the chances that they will be found by gray squirrels and chipmunks or white-footed mice. It also reduces the chances the jay will find them again. According to an article in *Natural History*, in less than a month a flock of fifty jays cached one hundred and fifty thousand acorns, 58 percent of the total nut crop from eleven pin oaks.

I left my yard and walked uphill to a clearing within sight of the oaks, where I could follow the birds' flight from the trees to the meadow and back. Whenever a jay left the oaks, its throat was distended and at least one acorn was visible in its mouth. For over an hour the jays collected and stored, then disappeared over the rim of Spaulding Hill, their voices falling away in the distance. A week before, a flock of jays had stripped the acorns from a small oak that grows in the meadow near our driveway, burying many in shallow holes in the lawn, and the rest in the woods beyond the driveway. Every spring a few red oaks sprout in the lawn, only to fall before the mower.

Like the ants with violet seeds, jays harvest only healthy acorns and beechnuts, and bury them just below the surface, a depth that favors germination. In a Wisconsin woodlot, blue jay–dispersed beechnuts had an 88 percent germination rate; those that fell from the tree sprouted only about 10 percent of the time. Since blue jays harvest and bury only soft-bodied nuts, this may be why oaks spread so quickly from their glacial refuge in the Southeast after the Ice Age.

According to a Virginia biologist, the rate at which oak trees migrated north ten thousand years ago surpasses even the advance of the red and white spruces with their light, wind-blown seeds. On average, wrote the biologist, oaks moved north 380 yards per year; the spruces, 270 yards. Spaulding Hill's blue jays, which travel miles between roosting and feeding sites, disperse both raucous calls and acorns. The distribution of red oaks in Blood Brook valley reflects the collective decisions made by communities of blue jays—selecting, dispersing, caching, retrieving—over the past century; the distribution of oaks across the northern deciduous forest represents an alliance between trees and jays over a period of time that exceeds human memory.

Gray squirrels, who generally get all the credit for being good foresters, have small territories and rarely store their nuts far from home. Along Blood Brook, I have seen gray squirrels only in the oak groves, never in our meadow or at our birdfeeders. That jays have wings makes all the difference. The large red oaks along the upper part of Bloodbrook Road, some more than a century old, may have been planted by jays.

It is birds, birds with tastes very close to my own, that propagate shrubs and trees all across the valley. Cedar waxwings, robins, bluebirds, catbirds, veerys, wood thrushes, and hermit thrushes are so indispensable to berry bushes—and consequently and inadvertently to my family's summer happiness—that the plants' fruiting strategy integrates the birds' need for food and the plants' need for seed dispersal. Waxwings prize Blood Brook blueberries and strawberries. They hop up from the unmowed lawn, their bills stained red, and fly to a maple limb to digest the sweet flesh of the fruit. The seeds pass unharmed through their intestines, then are defecated at some distance from its parent plant. This movement benefits the plant for two reasons. First, any seed germinating beneath the parent plant has to compete for light, water, and nutrients with mature members of its own species, plants whose roots are deeper, branches longer, and leaves fuller and more numerous than those of a germinating seedling. Second, because bird-dispersed seeds are scattered in small numbers, they are less likely to be eaten by seed-eating white-footed mice, which forage where seeds are numerous.

Casey, who celebrates his birthday at the height of the strawberry season, knows the waxwing only as a competitor. Someday he may appreciate that, like succession itself, the relationship between bird and berry and boy is circular.

To attract local seed dispersers and to cut down on wasted seed production (unpicked fruits rot on the stem or fall to the ground and become available to mice), some plants show preripening fruit flags; that is, the fruits go through a double color change before they mature. Green at first, such fruits become pink or red before turning a final color. Blueberries and blackberries turn pink before ripening; strawberries turn white, catching the eye of resident fruit-eating birds (and boys), alerting them to the imminent availability of ripe fruit. Some autumn-ripening fruits advertise their presence by leaf color. The leaves of wild grape, Virginia creeper, and poison ivy, vines that climb the trunks of deciduous trees along Blood Brook, change color to red and yellow about the time fall thrushes pass through the valley while the rest of the woods are still green. Like highway billboards, these colored leaves direct hungry migrants to sources of fast food; like harried tourists, these travelers do not have the time and energy, or familiarity with the local landscape, to search for their next meal.

The sequential ripening of fruits coincides with the energy demands of local or migrant birds. Summer fruits such as Juneberry, strawberry, blueberry, black raspberry, and blackberry are all high in carbohydrates and are eaten by resident birds. Fatty fruits such as the poison ivy berry ripen in the fall and are consumed for the most part by migratory birds, which need its high-lipid contents to fuel their migration. High-lipid fruits decompose faster than low-lipid fruits and must be eaten, if their seeds are to be dispersed, as soon as they ripen. Fall fruits that are high in carbohydrates and low in lipids, such as sumac, barberry, wild raisin, crab apple, and highbush cranberry, are bypassed by the migrants and remain on the plant for most of the winter. Slow to decay, they will be available to wintering birds and early spring migrants.

Sumac, the driest, fuzziest, least inviting fruit that I know, scorned all winter by scores of birds, becomes a March staple for pine grosbeaks and robins that, like kids, have eaten the more palatable foods first. These birds exercise their preferences through fall and winter, but, inevitably, if reluctantly, come to sumac in March, in a self-sustaining system that rewards producer and consumer, as well as observer.

Daddy Longlegs
and Mother Widows

I made my peace with spiders long ago. For many years our neighborhood movie theater sponsored a series of Saturday matinee horror shows, adolescent thrillers designed to twist pliable young minds from curiosity to dread. Among the scores of grade-B films I attended were two arachnid classics: *The Spider* and *Tarantula*.

Both films featured oversized spiders that preyed on people. In *The Spider*, a widowlike weaver bundles her victims in cable-thick silk and stores them in caverns filled with subterranean cobwebs. *Tarantula* hosts a great hairy thing that roams the Southwest ingesting innocent travelers, the creation of a mad physicist (played by Leo G. Carroll), who misuses radiation.

I took something home from both movies: nightmares. My bedroom became a haven for all of Long Island's imaginary spiders. Spiders carpeted the floor. Spiders collected on the walls, ceiling, and, horror of horrors, my bed. This was serious business

for a would-be naturalist. My fear of spiders was like a future doc-
tor's squeamishness at the sight of blood.

I overcame this phobia by getting to know a close relative of
the spider, the daddy longlegs, the stilt-legged, round-bodied
harvestman that lived in the well below my bedroom window.
The daddy longlegs has two especially appealing features: it
doesn't bite and it looks funny, like a sagging circus tent frame. It
is so fragile that a leg or two always breaks off when the creature
is roughly handled. It limps away to safety, its off-balance body
thereafter dipping precariously to one side. Between the ages of
seven and eight, I handled every daddy longlegs I found and left a
trail of severed legs in my path.

Next came jumping spiders. These attractive, half-inch spiders stationed themselves in full sunlight on the sidewalk or on
the shingles of my parents' home. A jumping spider is like an ani-
mated jumping bean; if you touch the end of its abdomen, it
jumps forward. Whenever a small fly or gnat settles close by, the
spider fastens a silk guy line to its perch, then springs off its
slightly modified fourth pair of legs several inches into the air. If
the spider scores, it bites the fly, picks it up, and backs into a
small crevice to enjoy a leisurely meal. If it misses, it retreats
along its guy line.

Two of the jumping spider's eight iridescent eyes are big and
convey an impression of invertebrate intelligence or, at the very
least, exceptional vision. The eyes of these active spiders are
among the most sensitive of all arthropods.

As an adult, I had a pet jumping spider, *Phidippus audax*,
named Cassidy. I caught her one September as she sunned herself
on a boulder close to our pond. Cassidy was quite attractive—
black with tiny white hairs and two rows of white dots along the
upper surface of her abdomen. Her eyes were iridescent purple,
her jaws, metallic green. She lived on a bed of silk in the mouth

of a spice jar. I fed her cluster flies and eventually released her on a windowsill where, on sunny winter mornings, she had a moveable feast at her disposal.

I have also made peace with orb weavers. One of my boyhood haunts, a vacant lot located down the block from my home, sported dozens of big black and yellow argiopes—what we kids called "garden" spiders. They seemed to appear out of nowhere in late summer, weaving their large and intricate webs among the meadow perennials. In fact, they were there all along, but in late summer as they fattened on increasingly larger grasshoppers and katydids, they too grew bigger and bigger and wove bigger and bigger webs.

I once watched another species of orb weaver fasten a guy line high in a hemlock and then swing across the driveway into a beech, like Errol Flynn. For reasons known only to the spider, it followed its line back to the hemlock, then walked upside down along its guy line, leg over leg over leg, two-thirds of the way back to the beech. It appeared to be walking on air. I lay down and watched its deliberate march above the driveway. The wind picked up. Its thread throbbed. But the indomitable spider, silhouetted against a sunset sky and shaking back and forth, inched forward. Then, three feet from the beech, its guy line snapped and the orb weaver swung back into the hemlock, an eight-legged Tarzan on a silken vine.

Around and around the hemlock branch it crawled, out to the end, front legs waving in the breeze like antennae. Then, the spider fastened a second guy line and rappelled eighteen inches. Suspended by its thread, it vibrated to the beat of the wind. Darkness thickened. The spider vanished into the evening.

Several months later, during a compulsive shopping spree at the local book store, I bought a paperback reissue of John Crompton's *The Spider*. Dawn spent in August meadows photographing dewy strands of argiope webs, tossing cluster flies into the dust-catching hovels that house spiders live in, even seeing reruns of *Tarantula* had taught me little about spiders. They deserved more of my attention.

When I opened the book I was not disappointed. Although some of Crompton's science is tenuous, his wit and verve are infectious and have turned me into a minor spider fanatic.

> It always seems to me that the lives of certain insects are more like plays than reality. And very good plays some of them are, particularly those staged by the bees, ants, and wasps. But of all the plays now running I am inclined to think that the one produced by spiders is the best. It has almost everything the modern audience wants: love interest, suspense, psychology, battle, murder, and sudden death.

Every fourth grader knows that a spider is not an insect. A few fourth graders may know that a spider is an arachnid, classified in the same phylum as an insect—*Arthropoda*—but different from them in having eight rather than six legs, two rather than three body parts (a spider's head and thorax are fused into a cephalothorax), and by lacking both wings and antennae.

A spider also has chelicerae, a pair of fanglike appendages in the front of the mouth which first puncture, then inject poison into its prey. The chelicerae make spiders ghoulish and fascinating. I can still see Leo G. Carrol's marbled eyes as he discovers that his little experiment has gone awry: that his irradiated, normal-sized tarantula has put on weight, busted out of the terrarium and laboratory, and is now stalking through the desert night, happily jabbing its chelicerae into the soft-skinned citizens of Winnemucka, Nevada.

In his book, Crompton explains the sequential steps a "typical" orb weaver takes to construct its web, using a series of diagrams marked with heavy lines and capital letters, reminiscent of a plane geometry text.

I learn that spiders have four to six spinnerets, small teats at the end of the abdomen from which the liquid silk issues, solidifying almost immediately after making contact with air. Each spinneret consists of up to six hundred small tubes, each with its own connection to a separate silk gland. (Later, after consulting another, more scholarly reference, I learn that spiders have up to eight spinnerets and usually less than a hundred tubes, or spigots.) Furthermore, spiders produce seven kinds of silk; all spiders produce three kinds, though none produces all seven, and that the tensile strength of spider silk is second only to fused quartz. As Crompton notes, "Frankly I do not know what fused quartz is. It is certainly not in use in the home. So if we are content to ignore this little known commodity we may say that spider silk is the strongest stuff that exists."

I don't know what fused quartz is either, but I discovered something when I was out inspecting spider webs one night. Five stout-bodied, hairy-legged female barn spiders had been building new webs each night under the overhang between the lights in the porch. Five brave little males lived there too, tucked in the recesses of their mates' webs. I turned on the lights and, with the aid of a hand lens, checked the closest web.

The web's spokes, radial lines to which tight concentric circles of silk were attached, were not sticky. I twanged a spoke. A spider came down. Each of the circles had minute droplets of glue spaced equidistantly all the way around. When I touched these, the silk lines stayed on my finger, and the glue stretched out like thin wisps of rubber cement. Again, the spider came down.

Why didn't each female spider stick to her own web? Crompton says spiders secrete oil on the bottom of their feet which allows them to walk on their webs without getting stuck. Too lazy to get cooking oil to verify this, I submerged my finger in the oiliest liquid on the porch, Casey's nontoxic Magic Bubbles.

I touched my wet finger to the web. At first, the lines stuck, then slid off as I withdrew my finger. Willing to believe Crompton's oil-on-the-bottom-of-the-feet theorem, I moved to an independent line of experiments. I took the Magic Bubble wand from the jar and began blowing bubbles into spider webs. Some stuck. Some didn't. One spider checked a bubble. A big, particularly grim-looking female touched the bubble with her two front feet, popped it, and retreated to the top of her web.

Later that night, I served this same spider a big moth, her preferred food and the reason barn spiders prosper beneath the outside lights. Stuck, the moth struggled in the web. The spider came. She bit it, twirled it around and around with her hind legs, all the while spraying the moth with a broad jet of silk. In the end, the comatose moth was hog-tied and cached with six others, all hanging like meat in a butcher shop from lines of silk.

Playing with the barn spiders teaches me other things. Despite its eight eyes, an orb weaver has poor eyesight; despite the ease of counting whippoorwill calls, there are other cures for insomnia; and that despite having turned forty, and despite some my best efforts, I'm still a little boy inside.

Barn spiders usually slow down in September. Mine stayed up by the porch lights, waiting at the edge of their webs each night; but by dawn they were sluggish with cold and heavy with dew. Although I left the lights on for a couple of hours the next night to attract moths, few showed up and none got caught in a web.

One cool September morning, I tapped a barn spider's guy line, the long, thick silk cord that runs from the spider's front foot across the web and attaches to the porch wall, eighteen inches below the web. Barn spiders use guy lines the way fly fishermen use rods; the slightest vibration of the guy line carries meaning. Instantly, the spider knows what is caught in the web—fly, moth, bee, grasshopper. Or its mortal enemy, a wasp, in which case the barn spider immediately cuts it free.

When I tapped a guy line in August, the spider rushed down the web, saw that nothing was fastened to it, and then returned to her position against the ceiling. On cool mornings when I tapped, her front foot jerked forward; that was all. The harder I tapped, the harder she jerked. Eventually, I began pulling the guy line in and out, working the spider like a puppeteer working a marionette. Except for her front leg, my spider was stiff, numbed by the September cold.

Because of the short growing season, northern New England barn spiders take two years to complete their life cycle. After their eggs hatch in late summer, the young disperse and hibernate. The next spring, they spin their webs in shady locations—barns, caves, overhanging cliffs, porches, and stone walls. They molt five to eight times, growing bigger with each molt.

When September returns, they drop into the leaf litter around the porch and hibernate. The following spring, their second year, they choose their web sites, fashion their webs, and feast on available flying insects. After his last molt, a male barn spider stops feeding and tears down his web. He then moves in with any female that will have him, spending the rest of his days tucked in a corner of her web, a sort of eight-legged Walter Mitty.

In late September, I can't find any male barn spiders on my porch. I think they've all starved to death or perhaps been devoured by their wives. Since male barn spiders become fatally anorexic after their last molt, their contribution to the next generation could, from an evolutionary standpoint, be nutritive as well as genetic without having an adverse effect on the neighborhood spider population. In an African species, the hatchlings devour their dying mother, leaving the web with both her genes and her digested remains.

Black widows are the most famous arachnid cannibals, but females of other spider species eat their mates, too. To avoid being victimized, male crab spiders bind their partners in silk before mating. Male wolf spiders perform elaborate dances, waving their front legs to signal their intentions. When the dance doesn't work the males are eaten.

My barn spiders were given a reprieve by the weather last fall when unseasonably warm air moved into the Connecticut Valley in late September and revived their food supply. After an absence of more than a week, moths and craneflies again gathered nightly around the porch lights, along with midges, gnats, and mosquitoes. Crickets and katydids sang louder and longer, their chorus paced by the warmth of the night.

With all this renewed activity, it's no wonder the barn spiders grew fat. As large as an inflated eight-legged nickel, each adult female barn spider rebuilt her web at dawn, having caught, tied, poisoned, and then sucked dry a sampling of the nighttime insect population. Only fragile husks remained of each meal. One spider grew so big with every feeding that an additional molt was necessary. I found a cast-off spider skin fixed to the porch ceiling like a glove to a clothesline.

Spiders were everywhere. During the first week in October, a jumping spider in the living room dangled onto my lap while I scanned the afternoon newspaper. A long-jawed orb weaver, the Twiggy of spiders, hung against the house by the edge of her narrow web. Her legs were pinched together, four pointing forward, four pointing backward in line with her abdomen. An unidentified spiderling dropped from the book shelf, another from the kitchen counter. One wandered across my open dictionary.

When I picked tomatoes and lettuce, I disturbed agile, ground-hunting wolf spiders. When I walked through the meadow, I disturbed goldenrod crab spiders. When I vacuumed windowsills, I disturbed American house spiders whose irregular, sticky webs—cobwebs if you prefer—gather dust and insects, and are a major line of defense against the flies of autumn.

Our uncut meadow again glistened with argiope webs. Fastened to purple asters and yellow goldenrods, argiope webs gathered both grasshoppers and dew. The center of each was decorated with thick, twisted strands of silk, resembling a vertical line of W's that warned sparrows and blackbirds away. Fastidious preeners, birds immediately remove spider silk from their feathers and learn to avoid the deliberately marked webs.

The horizontal web of a funnel weaver stretched eight inches across the tops of withered clover from my office wall to the stone steps. The spider lived in a silk funnel spun into the web. This web wasn't sticky, but the silk strands were woven so close together that the feet of any fly or cricket that landed on it got momentarily tangled. Funnel weavers are quick. Snug in her funnel, hidden between a board and tar-paper, she rushed to her prey to capture it before it could untangle its feet. Once caught, she dragged it back to her funnel and ate it at her leisure. Beneath her web, the victims' husks littered the ground.

Yet no matter how many spiders I found last October, the adults, at least, lived on borrowed time. When true October weather returned, their time was up.

Two mothers, both weighted by resolution, met on a summer afternoon. Neither one was prepared for what followed.

I first learned of the widows one summer, while I was away on assignment in South Dakota. Linny had found a large, satiny black spider on the hill in the meadow near our driveway, hidden under a large rock. "Yes," she said on the telephone, trying her best to sound casual, "there's a scarlet hourglass," meaning the legendary mark, which may be missing or indistinct or transformed into a couple of wavy lines on the belly of a female black widow.

I thought there was nothing to fear. Although he was two years old then and very inquisitive, Casey and all his day-care friends could never have overturned such a big rock and thus exposed their fingers to the most poisonous spider in the world. Unfortunately, this practical concern mattered little to a mother defending her child. Speaking from the Great Plains, I was too far away to provide genuine moral support and much too far to be spewing spider lore.

Several years before, a lumberyard in Windsor, Vermont, had donated a black widow to the local science museum. She was a big, hungry female that lived out her life incarcerated in a Ball jar, eating crickets, beetles, and flies. I guessed that the spider had hitched a ride on a shipment of wood from Massachusetts, like the huge, hairy tarantulas that show up from time to time on supermarket produce counters, having traveled north with the bananas.

Several months later, the museum's black widow died. Linny freeze-dried it in a vacuum freezer and then added the specimen to the museum's invertebrate collection. I promptly forgot about black widows until Linny rolled the rock over.

According to the *Audubon Society Field Guide to North American Insects and Spiders*, black widows, *Lactrodectus mactans*, range from Massachusetts to Florida, and west across the prairies to the California coast. Nowhere does the entry mention northern New England.

Recently, I spoke to a spider biologist. He told me that although they are associated with the South and are certainly much more abundant there, black widows are found all across the contiguous United States, and even in southern Canada. In the Northeast, they're restricted to natural solar collectors, the south sides of bared hills, often on the south side of large rocks where heat extends their season of activity.

This was precisely where Linny had discovered her. Our hill faces the sun, and just below the crest, where the snowplow turns around, is a swath of meadowland scraped bare by the plow. The stony soil heats fast.

Home alone with an energetic toddler, frightened and beset by visions of venomous killers, Linny felt compelled to act. She collected the spider, pickled it in alcohol, and shipped it to the Smithsonian for positive identification. Yes, indeed, it was a mature female black widow.

Her next move was, perhaps, the most aggressive thing Linny has ever done. She drenched the widow's lair with gasoline, then torched whatever might have been left of her family. She assumed that would be the end of the story, but she was wrong. The following summer, another widow fixed her web under the same rock.

Since female widows may live for three years, attaining full size their second summer, the new spider could somehow have escaped the holocaust or might have wafted there afterward. Like dandelion seeds, black widow spiderlings disperse on silk parachutes lofted by wind.

Proponents of Manifest Destiny, spiders spread and conquer. Shortly after leaving their silk egg case, black widow spiderlings scale nearby plants, and then cast out enough line to catch even the most subtle breeze. Those that land in suitable locales spin webs. Those that don't, die. In 1884, nine months after a volcano sterilized the small Indonesian island of Krakatoa, a spider returned to attach its web to volcanic cinder. The island's first sign of life since the eruption, it appeared months before the first plant seeded in.

Having dispatched the previous widows, Linny had plans for this spider, too. She sentenced her to life in a coffee can and placed the container with the spider and egg sac on a shelf in the woodshed. It was my spider now, she said. My problem, too.

In the 1902 edition of *The Common Spiders of the United*

States, James H. Emerton had this say about the black widow: "It's everywhere feared as poisonous and dangerous, probably on account of its large size and conspicuous colors, as there is no good reason for considering it more poisonous than other spiders." In an effort to make amends, a later edition of the book added this footnote: "It is now known that this spider, commonly called the black widow, is extremely poisonous; its bite has been known to cause death."

Every other book I have consulted is perfectly clear on the subject: the black widow is poisonous, the most poisonous spider in the Western Hemisphere, perhaps in the world. Drop for drop, widow venom is more potent than cobra venom.

In fact, both widows and cobras employ neurotoxins to subdue their prey and defend themselves against aggressors. According to *Black Widow*—the book, not the movie—symptoms of a widow bite were the very same ones I experienced the morning of my bar mitzvah: racing heartbeat, rising blood pressure, shallow breathing, slurred speech, and paralysis.

Several points should be kept in mind about black widows: they are timid spiders that prefer to retreat rather than to attack, and half of all black widows are the smaller, brown-, white-, and red-striped, nonpoisonous males. Most people who are bitten are bitten by mistake, often in outhouses. Since they fashion webs across privy seats to snare pupating flies that rise from the festering mounds of manure below, and since web-spinning spiders are practically blind, widows enthusiastically investigate any pressure against the web.

A California survey of black widow bites indicates that women are most often bitten on the hip or the buttocks, men on the tip of the penis. Visiting a southwestern outhouse now adds a new dimension to my desert trips.

Three weeks after Linny put the coffee can on the woodshed shelf, I opened it. The black widow lay on her back as still as stone. Both egg sacs had wrinkled and split. Suddenly a galaxy of light-colored spiderlings swarmed out, covering my fingers like a glove. I shook and slapped my hand and closed the lid.

Linny sentenced the spiderlings left inside the can to several months in a freezer. As a peace-making gesture, I searched the shed and woodpile, both prime sites for widows, and therefore for transparent spiderlings no bigger than mites. Although I knew that the babies were too small to be dangerous, a wave of foreboding swept over me as I thought about what next summer might hold.

In the Shadow
of Giants

Lulled by familiarity and habit, I often take second-growth woods along Blood Brook for granted, screening out woodland shapes, colors, and textures, much as I used to screen out city noise. Yet the legions of plants and animals which still live here reveal, if I really look, something of the nature of the largest, most complex deciduous forest the world has ever known.

Big trees remind me that, wither or wilt the petals, there is "no time to mourn roses, when forests burn," as Polish poet Juliusz Slowacki prophesied in the early 1800s; no time for a naturalist to mourn a tree that falls in the woods when whole species of trees—even the woodlands themselves—may cease to exist within coming decades.

Standing on my office porch in early December, looking northeast toward Spaulding Hill, dendritic origin of Blood Brook, I see the crown of a white spruce rising above scattered sprays of pine and a desolation of winter hardwoods. This tree has official as well as physical stature. It is the largest white spruce in the state of Vermont: 103 feet tall; 36 inches in diameter at breast height; and a 42-foot crown—a measurement that must have been taken some distance below the actual crown, because from my porch, the spruce appears perfectly straight, perfectly tapered, like a giant green arrowhead.

Big trees give me a sense of place and perspective in a world overflowing with the creations of humans. I am humbled by these trees, in awe not only of their size but of my own comparative insignificance, and I like the feeling. I am not alone in this response. Most conservation-minded people protest logging the old-growth Northwest, though abuse of the vanishing prairie gets less attention from them. Nearly every newspaper in America has a dossier on the spotted owl, a bird of the dark, dank 500-year-old hemlock and Douglas fir woods, yet has almost nothing to report about the black-footed ferret and northern swift fox, two endemic grassland predators whose tenure on Earth may be ended before the turn of the century.

The age of trees cannot be the only factor in our reverence for them, for every year several million tourists, ignorant of the nearby and older bristlecone pine, marvel at California's sequoias and redwoods. To bathe in towering green shade apparently means more than standing in the presence of living antiquity, for the oldest known living organism on Earth, a scrawny, eleven-thousand-year-old creosote bush, grows without fanfare in the desert Southwest. Eight thousand years older than the oldest sequoia, the China Lake creosote may have been browsed by mastodons and giant ground sloths, may have been watered by glacial meltwater that poured down the east slope of the Sierra Nevada at the end of the Pleistocene epoch to fill what are now desert valleys, and may have been momentarily cooled by the passing shadow of a teratorn, an extinct Ice Age vulture that was larger than a condor.

What is it about certain trees that so stimulates our imaginations? We like to be dwarfed, need to be dwarfed. It's comforting to take on the role of contributing team member, helpful, adaptable, but not necessarily essential to the outcome of the game, to reawaken as a utility infielder instead of a fire-balling pitcher, to see a giant tree rising out of the ground and know that it has been fashioned from sunlight, carbon dioxide, earth, and water, shaped by the winds and the seasons, and that it survives not because of me, but in spite of me.

Linny, Casey, and I visited the Spaulding Hill white spruce on a cold afternoon last winter. Six inches of fresh snow and a low, gray cloud ceiling compressed, condensed, and distilled both visibility and reality, as if the gap between ground and sky had narrowed.

Linny saw them first: three coyotes came up from the logging road, then barked, calling attention to themselves as they jogged between us, their nearly shapeless forms hidden by shrubs and saplings, animals the color and incarnation of that day. Without breaking stride, they moved east over Spaulding Hill, their echoes lingering behind them. Thrilled at the passing of the coyotes, we sobered quickly when we saw the spruce. Stepping beneath its circular sweep was like stepping into a circus tent; here, only a dusting of snow had reached the ground. Except for seedling spruce and ferns, little grew in the dense shade. Looking up the thick trunk into a progressively darker swirl of green and brown branches which eventually graded to black, I grew dizzy and disoriented. Dizzy and disoriented, the result of a single big tree, a specimen from my own home ground.

To get a sense of the primeval Blood Brook of four or five hundred years ago, I went to nearby Lord's Hill. The path from the old railroad bed climbed uphill for almost a mile, through brambles and legions of pole-sized red maple, through seemingly ordinary second-growth woods to a stand of white pine flagged with orange surveyor's tape. Walking past the pines, I entered a time warp: here were 25.7 acres of virgin hemlock and northern hardwoods—sugar and striped maple, basswood, white ash, hornbeam, beech, and yellow birch, the dominant association of trees which had once covered these rich, well-drained Vermont valleys and middle-elevation hills.

Along the northwest side of the hill, where the slope was almost level and the soil thick, rich, and poorly drained—a blend of glacial till and humus covered by a veneer of spongy, decomposing leaves—giant hemlocks, one over four hundred thirty years old, and yellow birch dominated in mixed and pure stands. Several of the birch were so thick that their characteristic bark—shiny yellow with horizontal lines, or lenticles, that peeled in thin curls—was thickened, furrowed, and fractured, making identification by bark alone difficult. Beyond the hemlock and birch, the land rose at a forty-five-degree angle. Here, the fecund earth supported the largest sugar maples I have ever seen. Two of the trees spread their crown more than a hundred feet above the forest floor and measured nearly five feet in diameter at breast height. Both trees had rooted in the hill more than four hundred years ago, a century before Sir Isaac Newton postulated gravity.

White ash, beech, and a smattering of basswood, yellow birch, balsam fir, and red spruce grew with the maples, and together formed a dense canopy that blocked the sun, shadowed the ground, and gave me the feeling I was walking through the woods described in a James Fenimore Cooper novel. Beneath the canopy, an understory of hornbeam and striped maple grew fifty feet tall and almost two feet thick at breast height, challenging my notion that understory trees are small. Carolina spring beauties and downy yellow violets carpeted the ground. I heard the hollow, directionless drum of a grouse.

A second stand of hemlock and yellow birch capped the virgin woods on Lord's Hill. Here, the soil was thin. Granite talus, deposited by glacial erosion, jutted from the earth, making walking hard. Tree roots reached over, under, and around rocks, spreading across the talus like woody snakes. One rock emerged from the lower trunk several feet above the ground, suspended by wood.

Visiting Lord's Hill was cathartic. I saw, for a few fleeting hours, the potential grandeur of a northern hardwood forest. When I look at the woods above Blood Brook, I can now imagine the size and shape of the trees when the Western Abenaki walked in their shade.

Last winter, Phoebe Bernadini, a forester friend, stopped to visit after a long day cruising timber on the west side of Spaulding Hill. She was tired, sweaty, and littered with scraps of the forest, but happy to work, having just graduated from the Yale School of Forestry with a passel of fellow students who called her Mom. Just before she turned fifty, Phoebe left her home and lover of twenty-five years, a daytime job as adult program coordinator at a science museum, and a life as renaissance moonlighter—potter, printer, house painter, beekeeper, market gardener, and assembler of computer hardware. She had bought land, built a house, attended school for two years, and overcome breast cancer. Short and gray-haired, Phoebe possesses a sophisticated sense of humor, sharpened by years of living within broadcast range of the Boston Red Sox, an infectious smile, and sparkling eyes. She shops at yard sales and drives a new Cherokee jeep with remote-control push-button ignition that she proudly starts while walking toward the vehicle. I inquired if she had seen the great spruce, the state champ, whose net of shallow roots drinks from the headwaters of Blood Brook and whose crown rakes the sky. She thought she had. Phoebe smiled as we walked out on the office porch to clarify the position of the tree, and then she started to laugh. She had considered the spruce old and diseased, had thought to herself that if it were cut, younger trees, dwarfed and suppressed by its shade, would quickly fill the hole in the canopy.

Central Vermont's trees make up a transition community between the boreal woods to the north and the temperate deciduous woods to the south. Dominated by sugar maple, American beech, yellow birch, and eastern hemlock, this forest also has white pine, white ash, basswood, butternut, red oak, red maple, black cherry, white birch, quaking and big-toothed aspen, red and white spruce, and balsam fir entering its overstory. On a short walk from the house I found them all "expressing themselves," as Phoebe says, each a miniature replica of its potential, like a crystal in solution which if left alone, slowly grows.

White pine tolerates well-drained, sandy, glacially minted soil like the deposits along the shore of Lake Fairlee and near the mouth of Blood Brook. White pines thrive, too, in abandoned fields, and on land flooded with sunlight as a result of being opened by fire, disease, or blowdown. Eventually, hardwoods will replace the pines, although this process takes several centuries. Along our driveway, a phalanx of pole-sized sugar maples grow in pine-shade, in water-retaining humus tempered by the slow decay of needles. I cut several of those pines last spring to encourage the maples. "Release them," Phoebe had advised.

Succession is a step-by-step replacement of one plant community by another, from open-field annuals to perennials to sun-loving shrubs and trees, and eventually to trees that reproduce in the shade of their own kind. This process illustrates the dynamic interplay of local geography, soil nutrients, and animals. Every community transforms its own environment and prepares the stage for the following community to take over, in effect committing ecological suicide.

Each species needs particular amounts of sun to perpetuate itself. The seeds of early successional trees such as big-toothed and quaking aspen, white pine, and gray birch need plenty of sunlight to germinate. These trees grow quickly and, except for white pine, are short-lived. After sun-loving trees have grown enough to make a little shade, red maple and red oak, which need less direct sunlight, can grow. Shade-tolerant trees eventually take over, but there are further successional trends within the dominant hardwoods. I find that light and tiny yellow birch seeds are usually the first to arrive and sprout in small forest openings. Next come the larger, whirling, winged samaras of sugar maple, and then the heavy nutlets of American beech, perhaps transported by a squirrel or a jay. If the soil favors beech, these nutlets sprout, eventually taking their place in the forest canopy. Sometimes a pure stand of beech develops in an otherwise mixed hardwood community where beech root suckers crowd out other species and spawn suckers of their own. Each tree in such a stand is a clone, an exact genetic replica of the original parent tree, a son of a beech.

"Climax" is the maladroit term used to refer to a once-supposed end point of plant succession, assumed to mean shade-tolerant sugar maples, American beech, yellow birch, and eastern hemlock in northern New England. Implying a constant linear progression, this image is more indicative of Western thinking than of ever-changing nature and many biologists dislike it. The pathways of succession circle, spiral, and radiate, continually sent backward, sometimes to square one, by local disturbances like fire, windfall, flooding, logging, and disease. Big trees are a reoccurring expression of a landscape in flux. On the geologic scale, they are as ephemeral as snowflakes.

White pine, a towering, long-lived transition tree, will keep coming back, its crown thrust above a sea of Spaulding Hill hardwoods.

Southeast of Lake Fairlee, less than a mile from the center of Bradford, New Hampshire, twelve enormous two-hundred-year-old white pines perch on a sandy knoll above the Warner River near a nine-hole golf course. These monolithic trees, the Bradford Pines, stand in lonely grandeur (adorned with lightning rods), relics of a wild and forgotten era when clouds of passenger pigeons roosted in their crowns, when men gathered in the woods with teams of oxen and crosscut saws, and when millions of great white pines ran down the sandy bluffs of New England's rivers toward the sea.

Two centuries ago, 200-foot white pines were not uncommon. A 240-foot specimen was dropped in Hanover on the site of Dartmouth College toward the end of the eighteenth century. In early summer, when the tiny male pine cones shed their pollen, golden grains were swept so far out to sea that British sailors thought the skies were raining brimstone. Today, white pine pollen, like windrows of beach sand, builds up along the shoreline of our pond, coats rain puddles, and rings red maples' trunks, marking spring high water in the swamp. In June, windshield wipers whisk away the botanical dust.

Colonial America was built from white pine, but unlike the Iroquois, who considered the pine the tree of life, settlers saw only its economic merits, and acted accordingly.

There is no greater account of cupidity in Northeast history than the raping of the pineries. Not even the slaughter of the beaver compares to the devastation of the white pine. When the colonists arrived in the land they called New England, stands of white pine extended from Massachusetts north to Newfoundland and west to the sandy shores of the Great Lakes. Much of Pennsylvania and New York south of the Adirondack Mountains was streaked with bands of white pine. Pioneers claimed that, except for crossing rivers, an ambitious squirrel (the animal so often used by early naturalists in evoking the pre-Columbian woods) could have traveled from Maine to Minnesota without leaving the branches of white pine.

The first sawmill in the New World was erected in York, Maine, in 1623, and from then on the attrition of the great pine forest continued unabated for nearly three hundred years. Fortunes were made on white pine. The light, soft wood floated easily, and it grew best in regions of heavy snowfall where oxen could drag logs over the snow to the river's edge for a run to market. Merchants set up a three-cornered trade: New England white pine logs were shipped to the west coast of Africa and exchanged for slaves, the slaves were traded in the West Indies for sugar and rum, and the sugar and rum were brought back to New England.

In 1691, with tall, straight white pine in such worldwide demand, the king of England worried that enemy sails would be rigged on American pine. John Wentworth, baron of New Hampshire pineries, was appointed surveyor general of His Majesty's woods in America. Wentworth was instructed to blaze the king's broad arrow—an R for Royal—on every big pine, thus reserving the tree for the English navy, and colonists were forbidden to cut trees broader than twenty-four inches in diameter. This proclamation was disputed and, like Boston's tea tax, contributed to colonial unrest. Clever, adroit Yankees sawed their pine boards no wider than twenty-three inches to avoid prosecution. When independence from the king was finally declared, profiteers leveled the pineries to help finance the revolution. As the king had foreseen, British ships were seriously handicapped by not having access to intact American white pine; the royal navy was forced to lash together broken pieces for masts.

After the war, white pine became the commodity on which some of the first great American fortunes were based, with that of the Wentworth dynasty of Portsmouth leading the way. By 1837 there were 250 sawmills on the Penobscot River and its tributaries above Bangor, Maine. Thoreau described ocean vessels held offshore for a week by mats of pine logs. Cincinnati was once held hostage by a three-acre logjam that contained more than 1.5 million feet of white pine. The longest haul of white pine was floated down from the tributaries of the Ohio River, two hundred miles north of Pittsburgh, to New Orleans, for a distance of about two thousand miles.

Around the Great Lakes, pines were cut for shingles. During a twenty-four-year period, eighty-five billion shingles were hand hewn in Michigan, Wisconsin, and Minnesota. Only the best wood was used for this, and more than 90 percent of each white pine was left to rot in the forest in testimony to the avarice of a developing nation that believed its natural resources were infinite.

The Blood Brook pine community represents at least the third coming of the white pine. At the height of the farming era, in the middle of the nineteenth century, more than 80 percent of the valley had been cleared. Then farming began to wane, pine seeded in the abandoned fields, and by 1900 ranks of pole-sized trees flanked the brook; twenty-five years later, they were tall enough to block the view. The Hurricane of 1938 tore them down again, leveling the pines on Bald Top and the east side of the valley—the east side of all the valleys, says Bill Godfrey, my ninety-one-year-old neighbor, who watched them fall like dominoes.

I marvel at the white pine, so straight and tall, remembering that its history is entwined not only with particular forests but also with all of the United States. In 1949 a pair of bald eagles fixed their nest to a white pine on the shores of Lake Umbagog in northern New Hampshire; then, after an absence of forty years from the state, another pair returned to the same tree to build again. The pine is the bald eagle of trees, a fitting symbol for a proud but reckless country that scavenges and pirates natural resources from all corners of the globe.

I want to know the secrets of the sugar maple in our front yard. I want to know how it survives a Vermont winter naked except for that thin robe of grooved gray bark. I want to know how it survives when the earth turns to stone and the wind drives snow and ice needles. And I want to know how next spring's sensitive new buds survive more than three months of on-again, off-again subzero weather, encased in soft brown scales.

One evening I nestled down with a plant anatomy book and discovered, much to my vexation, that there is no such thing as bark. Bark, said my reference, is a nontechnical term, a loose, ineffective word—like fish, or bug, or, for that matter, tree—that applies to all the tissue outside the vascular cambium. Besides leaves, flowers, and fruit, I recall vascular cambium as the only other part of a tree imbued with life, the principal food- and water-conducting tissues of a tree, a thin mesh of living cells known to botanists as a combination of primary and secondary phloem and xylem.

Phloem transports food up and down, xylem transports water. Primary refers to the initial growth and elongation sites at the tip of the maple's twigs and roots. Secondary refers to radial expansion, the maple's girth and the growth rings. If humans consisted of a veil of living cells under our skin and of clusters of such cells at the tips of our fingers and toes and head, we would be organized, cellularly speaking, like our front yard maple.

The outer secondary xylem, light-colored and alive, is called sapwood, the sap of which is bled from the maple. The inner secondary xylem, the heartwood, is an amalgamation of dead cells whose reserve materials have been leached to the sapwood. Heartwood, by far the bulk of any tree, is the framework on which the maple hangs its core. Heartwood resists gravity, holding the trifurcated trunk upright with its branches horizontal. Without it, the maple would be as limp as seaweed, for there would be no wood.

Bark, I discovered, is two distinct groups of cells: those alive and those not. The secondary phloem, conduit for transporting the maple's food, is synonymous with the inner bark. That is the reason girdling kills trees. Each year as my maple adds a new growth ring, a foamy layer of old secondary phloem cells is pushed to the outside. These cells die. The foam hardens into fatty, waxy substances filled with capsules of air. Botanists call this distinctive outer covering the rhytidome, which reveals the identity of each species of tree as songs reveal the identity of a bird. I call it bark. Regardless, it is the surface of a tree exposed to weather. As lifeless as a sweater, the bark or rhytidome is my maple's first line of defense against the cold and against the formation of internal ice.

Avoiding internal ice damage is the maple's biggest winter problem. How does a tree, any tree, which is more than 60 percent water, survive prolonged exposure to subzero temperatures? Like hatchling turtles, the tree supercools.

At −40 degrees Fahrenheit, ice forms spontaneously. As long as there are no dust particles to serve as nuclei for ice crystals, no ice will form until that very low temperature. The nearly pure water in the xylem and phloem cells of deciduous trees is supercooled to −40 degrees before freezing. In fact, the ranges of sugar maple, American beech, and yellow birch stop just north of the isotherm that indicates a winter minimum temperature of −40 degrees Fahrenheit. Beech endures a low of −42, sugar maple −45, and yellow birch −49. These slight differences in cold tolerance are attributed to the antifreeze properties of the respective trees' intracellular sugars, as a hike up Mount Washington confirms. With increasing altitude, deciduous woods yield to boreal. First beech, then sugar maple cease to grow. Yellow birch, the hardiest of the three, enters the lower end of spruce and fir zone, an ambassador from another realm.

In August the maple produces abscisic acid, a growth-inhibiting hormone that also increases the permeability of its cell membranes. With the first light frosts of September, the living xylem and phloem cells begin to release water into the intercellular spaces. When a hard freeze hits, ice crystals bloom in the intercellular spaces, and the unfrozen water in the cell cytoplasm migrates toward the frozen water outside the cell wall. As more and more water leaves, the cell shrivels like a deflated balloon, increasing the concentration of dissolved solids within the plasm membrane. And the higher the concentration of dissolved solids, the lower the freezing point.

Ice crystals often rupture the outer, stiff cell wall, indenting but not puncturing the inner, elastic plasma membrane. If the bottom should fall out of the mercury, however, and temperatures drop below the maple's threshold, as often happens on the cutting edge of a tree's northern range, ice would form inside the cells. When the plasma membrane ruptures, the cell dies. When too many cells die, the tree dies.

Some northern trees freeze-dry their cells by removing almost all the cytoplasmic water until huge crystalline masses of ice crowd the intercellular spaces. Paper birch, whose trunks reflect winter sun like fresh snow, and the scrubby red osier dogwood that crowd the open wetlands along Blood Brook, can survive submersion in liquid nitrogen at −321 degrees Fahrenheit. I remember watching Mr. Wizard tap a tulip dipped in liquid nitrogen against the corner of a table, shattering the flower into hundreds of pieces that flashed before the television screen like splintering ceramic.

With the unlocking of spring, intercellular ice melts, water is sucked back through the plasma membrane into the maple's cells—

hence, into the sap bucket—and normal metabolic processes resume. Now, the tree is no longer cold hardy, and even a minor spring freeze can damage it.

Even blindfolded, I would know if I stood beneath towering hemlocks. I might be on the north side of Spaulding Hill, or in Indiana's Turkey Run State Park; in the Wisconsin Dells, along the Bronx River in the New York Botanical Gardens; in the Smoky Mountains of North Carolina or the Alabama Hills; or I might be on wind-swept Cape Breton Island, Nova Scotia. The drone of motor vehicle traffic may fill the background and exhaust fumes may dominate the air, but when I step below the hemlocks, I step into cool, dark, moist woods, whose microclimate is remarkably similar no matter where it grows. And if I stood under Spaulding Hill's hemlocks in June, I would be sure to hear the slow, dreamy song of the black-throated green warbler.

Bonsai hemlocks suppressed by green overlords near the head of our driveway may be fifty years old, Phoebe told me, and like goldfish would resume their youthful vigor if given room to grow. Freed from competition, they would grow taller and wider, she explained; the older a tree is when released, the faster it responds to new freedom. Some understory hemlocks wait tenaciously for more than a century before rising toward an opening in the canopy.

Phoebe has studied the hemlock's biology and sees her work according to a hundred-year game plan. Hemlocks are slow-growing, long-lived, and large: the record age for an eastern hemlock is 988 years; the record height, 160 feet. The stoutest hemlock recorded was more than six feet thick, but suppressed trees an inch in diameter may be a century old. What one generation of foresters manages the next generation harvests.

Who among us looks so far into the future? Who among us cares?

In September 1985 an augury of death swept over the eastern hemlock, when Hurricane Gloria whisked woolly adelgids, an Asian insect, across Long Island Sound and into Connecticut. Adelgids do not destroy Asian hemlocks, but they level eastern hemlocks. Like mosquitoes, the tiny, fuzzy larvae drain sap from twigs and young branches, feeding close to the needles' attachment point. By feeding in late winter and early spring, they retard or curb the soft green flush of new growth and cause the existing needles to dry out, discolor, and eventually to drop. Large limbs die the first summer, the entire tree within a year. I worry about the woods of Blood Brook, and the integrity of the northern deciduous forest, for although adelgids have not yet reached Vermont, they continue to press north. Foresters stand hollow-eyed and haggard as the eastern hemlock joins a growing group of beleaguered New England trees—red spruce, American beech, white ash, and sugar maple, all recently infected with host-specific diseases.

Driving home from Casey's day-care center, I pass the largest, most beautiful American elm on Thetford Hill. It stands alone, abreast of the road, dwarfing a white farmhouse. A fluid tree, curiously and gracefully feminine, the trunk forks into sweeping branches that rise obliquely, divide repeatedly, then droop down, giving the elm the appearance of a green, gushing whale spout. Because of its size—a recent inventory of big trees listed it as Vermont's fourth largest American elm—I notice it, and because I notice it, it speaks to me, suggesting two conflicting messages or, perhaps, a single message with two meanings.

The first message is crisp and clear: How fragile the life on Earth. In the late 1920s, shipments of elm veneer logs arrived in the United States from Europe with an unexpected passenger: *Ceratocystis ulmi*, a host-specific fungus that is carried by bark beetles. In this land of many elms, the fungus spread from eastern ports of entry, west along railroad rights-of-way, escorted on its journey by the immigrant European elm bark beetles, which were discovered in Boston in 1909 and which essentially displaced the American elm bark beetle. The fungus, known as Dutch elm disease, was first diagnosed in Ohio in 1930.

Everywhere, elms died. According to Bill Godfrey, Blood Brook's elms died off in the mid-1970s. Then, there is the elm's second message: Death bears life. The recent increase of pileated woodpeckers in northern New England coincides with the spread of Dutch elm disease. All the three broods of woodpeckers I have watched were born in the trunks of barkless elms. A year after the woodpeckers nested, one cavity housed a kestrel, another a saw-whet owl. And a study of Ohio salamanders found that red-backed salamanders, among the most common vertebrate species in the Northeast, avoid the summer sun by hiding under piles of rotting elm bark, a rapidly increasing microhabitat.

Between Blood Brook and our pond stands a dead elm. During the last three years, storms have broken off all but the four stoutest limbs. Downy woodpeckers excavated a nest cavity in a snag last year, and white-breasted nuthatches use it now. The elm has also sponsored a family of southern flying squirrels and fledged two broods of tree swallows. It is the perfect lookout for raptors. One April night, while I lay by the pond searching for spring peepers, a barred owl landed in the elm. I shut off my headlamp and for several minutes watched the owl caterwaul, silhouetted in moonlight. Another owl answered, eight hollow-sounding hoots, like the bark of a distant dog. Silently, the first owl departed, passing directly over me, a mouse or a shrew pinioned in its bill. I have seen broad-winged hawks hunting garter snakes from the elm, sharp-shinned, red-tailed, and red-shouldered hawks, a goshawk, the pair of turkey vultures that came to a deer carcass I set below the tree, a great blue heron, three ravens, and many crows. It is a whippoorwill podium, a cedar waxwing berry-scouting post. Every day, blue jays, purple finches, and chickadees pause there before coming to our birdfeeders.

I know the systematic death of the American elm has been a boon to wildlife. But this is a short-term benefit, I suspect, for eventually the dead elms fall and the piles of bark rot. Which brings me full circle. An anachronism, the Thetford Hill elm reminds me that a seemingly inconsequential event, importing veneer logs from Europe, affected an entire biological province, for American elms were once abundant in valleys and flood plains, on lawns and city streets from Cape Breton to eastern Saskatchewan and south to Florida and central Texas, almost the breadth of the pre-Columbian deciduous forest. If wisdom comes with age and experience, because of our relative youth as a species we can claim no privileges. Who can imagine life without a rainforest? Or life with diminishing biologic diversity?

In 1975, when I moved to northern New England, I was surprised to find American chestnut sprouting like cowlicks from stumps in southern New Hampshire. By all historic accounts, I live at the northern edge of the chestnut's range, which formerly ran from central New England west to Illinois and south to the Gulf Coast. Chestnuts had followed the warmer river valley north, possibly even to Fairlee. Then the infamous blight of 1904 reduced chestnuts from towering canopy trees that dominated much of the temperate deciduous forest to unruly understory sprouts.

Last winter I visited a big American chestnut that grows on the edge of a pasture in Ely, near the north end of Lake Fairlee. Several buckets' worth of burrs littered the ground. Since male and female flowers ripen at different times, preventing chestnuts from self-pollinating, without another mature tree nearby, this one's thin, shriveled nutlets remain infertile, bounded in prickly jackets that protect them from squirrels, which feed elsewhere.

The origin of the Ely tree is a mystery. A chestnut pathologist from Connecticut believes that east-central Vermont is not part of the native range of the American chestnut, and therefore the tree had to have been planted sometime in the last century, a once common practice that extended the chestnut's distribution west to Wisconsin and even Oregon. The tree's current owners claim the Ely chestnut seeded in during the tenure of the previous owner, a Vermont hill farmer who told them that the tree had grown there as long as he could remember. One thing I'm sure of, this is the largest chestnut I have ever seen.

How does the Ely chestnut survive? Is it immune to the chestnut blight, which leveled forests, or were there just too few chestnuts in east-central Vermont to support the blight?

At the beginning of the twentieth century, every fourth tree in the hardwood forests of the central Appalachian Mountains was a chestnut. No other nut-producing tree, not even all the species of oak or hickory collectively, had inspired as spirited a following as the chestnut which brought the flocks home to its shade. The nut crop, annual, dependable, and huge, fed wild turkeys, black bears, white-tailed deer, foxes, gray squirrels, opossums, and raccoons. People ate chestnuts, ate the animals that ate the chestnuts, and employed chestnut wood for almost everything from cradles to coffins, as the wood split with straight grain, worked easily, and was resistant to rot.

During the summer of 1974, I was a naturalist at Cumberland Gap National Historic Park, a small park—about twenty thousand acres—that straddles the Virginia-Tennessee-Kentucky border. Among my duties was leading bird walks to the tri-state border, where, during lulls in the morning, I would demonstrate how to put one's appendages in three states simultaneously. History-rich Cumberland Gap park pursued "living history" as part of its interpretive programs. Beginning with Dr. Thomas Walker's "discovery" of the gap as he was tracing a bison and elk trail west, and followed nineteen years later by Daniel Boone and company's historic pilgrimage on Wilderness Road, the park showcased the history of the area, with a renovated nineteenth-century Appalachian hilltop settlement as its focus.

To properly interpret the settlement's history, the park service provided costumes, wigs, and clip-on beards. Except for the clothes, I already looked the part: full bushy beard and wild, unruly hair that sprouted from under my hat like chestnut saplings from a stump. Unfortunately, I had to cut my own hair and beard and wear theirs.

The entire settlement attested to the importance and abundance of American chestnut: the buildings, the shingles, the furniture, the split-rail fences, the corrals. Tannin from the bark was used to cure leather. Weathered moonshine stills burned chestnut wood because the smokeless flame did not alert prohibitionists in the valley below. There was even a leafed-out forty-foot American chestnut growing in a pasture near the settlement, at that time the largest living chestnut I had ever seen. Flagged with orange surveyor's tape so that the maintenance crew who mowed the pasture would spare the tree, the chestnut had a small, lollipop crown, nothing approaching the Ely tree.

Although the chestnut blight had reached Virginia fifty years before, its devastation looked fresh, for barkless trunks still stood like grave markers across the otherwise green Cumberland Mountains. Fallen trees, slow to rot, dented the forest floor. Everywhere bouquets of scrawny chestnuts continued to sprout from stumps, reaching about twenty feet in height and dropping infertile nuts before dying of blight.

I still have a score of American chestnut leaves, collected that summer, pressed between the pages of a dictionary. From time to time, I open to a leaf. And remember.

The blight, *Cryphonectria parasitica*, a fungal noose that garrotes chestnut trees but never enters the roots, grows completely around the cambium layer of a stem or branch or trunk, preventing the flow of water and nutrients past the point of infestation, killing whatever grows above. Infected saplings die in months, towering trees in a few years.

Infected American elms also die by self-induced starvation as they attempt to stop Dutch elm disease. Pushed by rising sap, fungus spores spread rapidly through the tree's vessels. To protect itself from further infection, the elm plugs the diseased vessels, blocking the further spread of spores. Diseased branches wilt, leaves fall, and dried twigs crack in the wind. Since bark beetles continue to transport the fungus to healthy limbs, an elm with a beetle infestation may die of thirst in a month.

The chestnut blight arrived in the port of New York with nursery stocks of Asian chestnut trees around the turn of the century and was first detected in 1904 on the American chestnuts that lined the walkways of the Bronx Zoo. The blight did to the American chestnut what smallpox did to the American Indian. Swift and lethal, it felled whole forests, nations of trees. Over the next fifty years, fungal spores were spread by wind, birds, and insects, and every native chestnut stand in eastern North America had bowed under the blight as if it were an illwind from the Old Testament. The specter of these gaunt chestnut forests remained.

Although plant pathologists have recently isolated strains of nonvirulent blight which graft to and render harmless the lethal forms, the American chestnut will probably remain subservient to the trees that have grown in its place, or relegated to a curiosity like the Ely chestnut. I ache to comprehend a species' swift demise, and measure carefully our future.

The Color
of October

One October dawn when the valley was a carnival of color, I
drove down Middlebrook Road toward Lake Fairlee. I must have
been the first car on the road for some time, for a red fox was
curled across the double yellow line, sleeping. As I approached,
the fox fled.

Farther down the road, a coyote crossed a pasture, heading
for the line of alders which follows Middle Brook up the valley
from the lake. I stopped to watch. Without breaking into a trot,
the animal picked up his pace, paused, cocked his head over his
shoulder, and, glancing askance at me, disappeared in the alders.

His color mirrored the hillside maples, which were not nearly
as bright as the fox but orange nonetheless. An October coyote,
indeed.

Color comes to Blood Brook in early September, crescendos
in mid-October, and fades by November. What is color, really?

Senescent leaves. The byproduct of water conservation. Summer's funeral pyre. An expression coined by some taciturn Yankee for the chromatic miracle that starts with the lighting of the arboreal vine Virginia creeper and travels from tree to tree, from branch to branch, until a blaze erupts, first in the valley, later in the hills. Color spreads to roadside sumac and to swamp maple. By early October, Spaulding Hill and Bald Top are kaleidoscopic. Sugar maple and white ash change color by the hour.

After the last russet oak turns brown, the riot ends. Except for the beech and red oak, which hold some of their leaves all winter, and the bone-white birches, by November Blood Brook's deciduous woods are as gaunt and gray as the North Atlantic.

It's easier for me to speak of the physiology of color, the how and why of it, or to record its progress from valley floor to stony hill, than to describe the rich and varied hues. Perhaps only a painter can do that, someone who works with the difference between mahogany and russet, between mauve and maroon, between burnt ocher and burnt sienna.

Every October, to convey both an essence of local geography and the nuances of color that make Spaulding Hill, Blood Brook valley, or the front yard maple different from all others, I tell Casey a home-grown story, borrowed from several Native American myths and a European folk tale, and spiced with a personal touch. Although plant physiologists may not necessarily agree with this story, they cannot deny that the land grows myths as well as trees.

There is a great bear that travels across the sky, dipping toward Earth in late September.

Once, a long time ago, when Earth was young and perpetually green, the bear lived on land. He was pursued, day after day, by a giant warrior, until finally the warrior caught up with the bear. He grabbed the bear by his short, stubby tail and swung him around and around, faster and faster, stretching the bear's tail as he hurled him head over heels into the night sky.

The bear still wanders the northern sky, circling. (We know him as the constellation *Ursus major*, the Big Dipper.) And for as long as anyone can remember, celestial warriors have stalked the sky bear. Each autumn the warriors get closer than they do the rest of the year.

They follow the bear, hoping to catch and cook the beast before the snows of winter end the hunt. Being a slow learner, the bear makes the same fatal mistake every year: he grows thirsty in the autumn and travels down the sky vault, close to Earth, to sip the northern lakes before they freeze. The first warrior, robin, catches up to the bear and pierces him in the side with an arrow. Blood gushes from the wound, spreading across the hills and wetlands, staining the leaves of maple and sumac and blueberry. Robin and his cousin, bluebird, cannot avoid the red flood, and to this day their tribes wear the color of the kill upon their breasts.

Blood hits the Virginia creeper and poison ivy, then the plumes of sumac, and spreads to the swamp maple. Then it seeps to the huckleberry and viburnum, the blackberry and cinquefoil. When the bear is quartered and bled, the hills are washed in red, staining the sugar maple and red oak, even the berries of the Jack-in-the-pulpit and ginseng.

Next the second warrior, chickadee, prepares the pot for the great feast by heaping mounds of yellow fat in the cooking vessel, which soon begins to hiss and spit. The overflow reaches Earth, coloring the as yet uncolored trees. Brightest of all are the aspens, which tremble and flash in the October sun. Yellowed, too, are the elms and the cottonwoods, the witch hazels, the larches, and the birches. And in the deep woods, even the beech and striped maples.

The third warrior, gray jay, is late; he arrives after the kill and after the work. "The lazy hunter," the jay will forever follow the others, begging for table scraps.

The great bear has been slain. The three warriors have feasted. Throughout the long nights of the fall and winter, the bear's skeleton lies on its back in the sky, and the trees that were touched by his magic stand like bones: together, the bear and the trees lie stark and mute.

Each spring life returns to the trees and to the bear, who rises with the sap to be chased by the warriors yet again. Each autumn, just beyond the equinox, as the corpulent beast grows thirsty, he is caught, butchered, and bled, his fat rendered and spilled. With the carnage comes the color, grist for the mythological mill.

I cannot visualize plant cells, hundreds of millions of busy cells preparing for winter. Yet the scientific explanation for fall foliage, clinical counterpart of my bear story, also contributes to my understanding of how the trees, the land, and the climate collaborate in one grand, mutable color wheel. Subtle decreases in the amount of daylight trigger even subtler changes in tree chemistry, changes essential to the tree's winter survival; fall foliage follows. But by this account color is superfluous, a by-product of winterizing which has no value to the tree. Perhaps the only ones to notice and assign meaning to the metamorphosis of the hills are we humans and a few species of migratory, fruit-eating songbirds.

Through the opulent days of early October the woods glow brightly with dying leaves as the air, crisp and pungent, runs like a brook. There's less humidity than in summer and more light, for curtains of yellow leaves reflect the lowering, flattening beams of sunlight. Everywhere, color intensifies. Bluebirds look bluer; foxes, a deeper, richer orange. These are the days of luminous spider lines, when ground fog stalks the hills and geese traverse the sky.

The red maples at the south end of Lake Fairlee are red, their color triggered by decreasing daylight, the shifting photoperiod, one constant to which biological clocks can be set since it occurs year after year at the same time. Don't believe the tales about Jack Frost painting fall color across the Northeast. Frost ruptures plant cells, and their contents leak. Hard frost kills color.

A week later the yellowing leaves of our front yard sugar maple have a brown edge to them, indicating frost damage. One fall the tree began turning in early September. By Labor Day weekend, 20 percent of its leaves showed traces of yellow and orange. Two weeks later, those leaves had fallen, and half of the remaining leaves were yellow, mostly on the top and along the outer branches. When a hard frost followed, what was yellow became brown and what was brown dropped off. The next year, almost the entire tree was yolk-yellow at once. One morning, just before the sun climbed into view, I photographed frost patterns along the outer edges of the maple's leaves. The air was still, windless. Perfect for slow shutter-speed photography. Then the sun rose, loosening the frost. Yellow leaves fell all at once.

Color conserves water and recycles nutrients. Chlorophyll, the green pigment in leaves, captures energy from sunlight. Using it to fuel the combination of carbon dioxide and water, chlorophyll produces a simple carbohydrate, glucose, basic food for the tree and the forest. But chlorophyll is volatile. Sunlight destroys it. A constant supply of water up through the trunk and into each leaf is required for the tree to continue manufacturing chlorophyll. No chlorophyll, no photosynthesis. No photosynthesis, no food production.

Throughout the spring and summer, water travels from the maple's roots to its leaves, replenishing the chlorophyll spent during photosynthesis. Most of the fluids that travel into each leaf are transpired from tiny openings, called stomata, on the leaf's undersurface. Each leaf is a conduit between earth and sky. Forty apple trees transpire about sixteen tons of water a day! Our sugar maple, along with every deciduous tree in the valley, sheds its leaves in October to cope with the five and a half months of drought that winter brings. With more than a quarter of a million leaves—enough says Rutherford Platt, author of *The Great American Forest*, to carpet a half acre—and with more than a hundred thousand stomates for every square inch of leaf, a transpiring sugar maple could never replenish its winter water losses, for its roots are sealed off from surface moisture. Even when snow melts, very little moisture percolates through frozen ground, so the water runs off rather than into the soil. Our maple, if fully leafed out in winter, would choke as surely as if it were rooted in arid Tucson.

The maple's passage to fall color starts during the lazy days of high summer. Although July leaves look green and stable, subtly decreasing amounts of daylight trigger the beginning of nitrogen reabsorption or translocation, from the leaves back into the tree's woody tissues. Some potassium, phosphorous, sulfur, magnesium, and manganese are also translocated. We cannot see this process. We can't hear it or feel it. But by early October, more than half of each leaf's nitrogen and phosphorous has been metabolized into woody tissue, where it acts as an antifreeze for the tree and provides an infusion of nutrients for early spring growth. Temperate deciduous trees need tremendous amounts of nitrogen and carbohydrates to leaf out and begin to grow each spring, and some trees along Blood Brook—red maple and shadbush, for example—cast flowers before leaves. Without translocation, where would the building blocks of life come from? The ground is frozen all winter, fallen leaves unable to decompose idle in the snow, and photosynthesis shuts down in October. Translocation provides the efficient and essential answer, for the rising spring sap carries the juices necessary for growth. Water-soluble calcium is the only mineral element of any consequence remaining in the leaves that fall to the ground. Color, then, is the result of water conservation and nutrient translocation, the aftermath of high-tech leaf chemistry.

How can anyone be jaded when the hills are covered with wine-red maples? Every fall the change is drastic and dramatic. Green becomes yellow. Becomes orange. Becomes purple. And when wind loosens leaves, color tumbles.

When I was a boy, I wanted to see the precise moment Long Island's hickories and sweet gums went from green to yellow and scarlet. In September, I would remind myself to look, be patient, be observant. As weeks passed, diversions mounted: a Yankee pennant race, for example. In the brief time my pledge was forgotten, color would steal into the schoolyard trees. Suddenly, as though awaking from a dream, I'd see the warm hues of autumn everywhere.

Yet my boyhood suppositions notwithstanding, color does not arrive overnight. Cool September nights stimulate cells at the base of the leaf stem, or petiole, to dry out. Just inside these cells a layer of tough, corky cells develops, stopping the flow of water into the leaf, stopping the export of carbohydrates and metabolic waste back to the tree. With the flow of water staunched, the production of chlorophyll stops. The leaf is isolated from the tree. As chlorophyll wanes, lesser pigments appear; some have been obscured all summer by overwhelming green; others form in the cell sap by the recombination of simple sugars and leaf waste products that cannot exit through the barrier of corky tissue. Yellow. Gold. Red. Orange. Copper. Mahogany. Purple.

The emergence of these hues signals the approaching death of deciduous leaves. Yellow xanthophylls, the pigment so abundant in egg yolk and butter, and carotene, the pigment in carrots, both of which are present in varying amounts in different species of trees all summer but hidden by chlorophyll, transform to golden yellow the leaves of American elm and quaking aspen, paper birch and black willow.

This is simple mathematics, explains Edwin Way Teale, in *Autumn Across America*. Autumn yellows are produced by subtraction, the subtraction of chlorophyll; autumn reds by addition, the addition of sugars and leaf wastes, which cannot exit through plugged petioles.

Anthocyanin yields the red of sumac and blueberry and Virginia creeper, the blue of white ash, the purples of viburnum. If the leaf sap containing anthocyanin is acidic, leaves turn red. If the sap is alkaline they turn blue or purple. Anthocyanin is a sun pigment. After the corky cells isolate the leaf from the tree, bright sunny days use up the remaining chlorophyll and stimulate the production of anthocyanin. Blood Brook's sugar maple leaves turn yellow in the shade, red in the sun, and, depending on the proportion of sun or shade, and on genetics, they change hourly from yellow to red to orange. Leaves in the sun turn red, and red moves from the top of the tree down and from the sides in. The higher the content of sugar trapped in the leaves, the more brilliant the color.

If early October is overlaid with clouds, little anthocyanin is produced. Leaves go from green to yellow. Sunny days and cool nights generate reds and oranges and purples. An abundance of sugar maples, which contain in their leaves all three pigments—xanthophyll, carotene, anthocyanin—gives the northeastern United States the most outstanding foliar pageant on Earth. Along Blood Brook, as go the sugar maples, so goes fall color. With lots of bright sun, the Blood Brook maples are outrageous: yellow branches one day, orange the next. Each leaf has its own pattern. Yellow spreads from the leaf margins inward. Green retreats to the veins. Soon, the veins turn yellow. Then, orange appears along the leaf margins, replacing yellow. Finally, the whole leaf is orange, dusted with red, inlaid with yellow. Yet if shelves of clouds hide the sun, the maples brighten only to yellow. And heavy October rain will leach the leaf pigments, washing away color.

Although the sugar maple gets credit for the most lavish run of color, the white ash strikes a vivid cameo. Alkaline cell sap in ash leaves causes anthocyanin to purple rather than redden, contrasting with carotene and giving the tree an incandescent appearance. In bright October sun, the big ash by my office produces anthocyanin, rimming the tree in mauve. Because the inner leaves receive less sunlight, they shine with the bright yellow of carotene. Standing beneath the tree, looking straight up, I follow the yellow as it spreads up and out, grading to purple where leaves meet sun, glowing with a soft, cellular radiance. There is nothing else like white ash in the Northeast.

The outer compound ash leaves, which change from green to yellow to purple, have a beauty all their own. Wherever leaflets lay against each other, blocking sunlight from the shaded portion, wedges of yellow carotene cut across the purple, forming intricate geometric designs. Overlapping sumac leaflets do the same thing, but because of acidic cell sap, their compound leaves produce bold red and yellow patterns.

Not all deciduous trees are radiant. Brittle butternut leaves drop as soon as the corky cell layer forms, leaving the tree naked while the rest of the woods shine. Locust leaves fall off while still green. Apple, sycamore, and white oak merely lose their chlorophyll, and become paler and paler, eventually turning brown. Tannin, the pigment in the leaf cells of these trees, contributes a light brown color to the autumn hills. Beeches are duotone. With both tannin and carotene in its leaf cells, beech leaves are a rich tan with golden veins, and sometimes the two colors blend to make mahogany.

Although deciduous trees are found throughout the world,

only in eastern North America, particularly in northern New England and New York's Adirondack Mountains, is autumn color so intense. Europe has deciduous forests, as do the east coast of China and the west coast of Chile, and these regions get color too, though neither as bright nor as inspiring as ours. England's mild, often cloudy fall weather stifles the production of anthocyanin. Blood Brook's hills and valley shine in autumn because of a perfect blend of weather and of chilly nights and sunny days, and because sugar maples dominate. Without either, autumn would be yellow.

Standing on Bald Top, the creases and folds of eastern North America stretching before me, I imagine a front of color moving south to the tall timbers outside Tallahassee, west to Manitoba's Red River, a thousand miles in either direction. It ranges from the cranberry bogs of Cape Cod, to the Catskill Mountains, to crimson tupelo and flashing sweet gum in New Jersey's Pine Barrens, tracing the meandering lines of yellow silver maples that follow the Hudson, the Susquehanna, the Ohio, the Mississippi, the James, and the Tennessee, passing over dull red chestnut oaks that run the crest of eastern Pennsylvania's Kittatinny Ridge. Every geologic ripple on the land—the Holyoke Range, the Pocono Mountains, the Allegheny Plateau, the Blue Ridge Cumberland Pass (where Daniel Boone surely paused to admire the color), the Great Smoky Mountains, the Ozark Plateau, even the southernmost bumps of the Appalachian Mountains in northeastern Alabama—has its individual pockets and patterns of color. Instead of going west, Teale should have gone south with autumn, riding the colored waves down the Appalachian chain, up the hills and down the valleys from Maine's Baxter State Park to Stone Mountain, Georgia.

I've looked at enough Octobers in the West to know that they're not the same. As a break from graduate school, I used to hike the wild, unpeopled Sangre de Cristo Mountains northeast of Santa Fe, New Mexico. Mountainsides of yellow aspen flanked by aquamarine Englemann spruce thrust into a blue western sky. Although inspiring, there was clearly something missing. The following fall, I traveled east from Vancouver on the Canadian National Railroad. Alone and depressed as I crossed the bleak beef belt, I saw splashes of red, then patches of red, on the horizon. Immediately, I perked up. By western Ontario, I was euphoric, for the woods above Lake Superior were colored, mostly red with suggestions of yellow. I was back East. In autumn. I was home in the land of the sugar maple.

The genius of one maple is worth an entire hillside of aspen. It's like comparing Mozart to Manilow. Aspen is yellow, yellow only, whereas maple is moody, unpredictable, its colors an ephemeral reflection of the weather. They cannot be spoken. They're too varied, too rich, too unstable.

On the south end of Lake Fairlee, watery reflections condense and distill and distort an autumn landscape. Reflections are selective: like a dream they gain perspective by filtering frivolous details, blackening edges, intensifying colors and textures until an image floats alone. As though seen through a telephoto lens, a reflection concentrates in focus, one aspect heightened, another softened. Background disappears. Foreground blurs. And like a photographic image, a reflection is inverted, often out of context.

The maples on the south end of the lake tint the water, salmon pink against a galaxy of black. There's depth here. This is not a simple mirror image that can be peeled off the water like a steamed postage stamp. It is three-dimensional and profound. To photograph them, I focus my camera below the surface, into that black hole where reflections grow, where water bends light and twists reality.

Ospreys know these depths. Talons extended, one plunges through October into Lake Fairlee's western bay and impales a fish.

Vigil with Pileateds

I hadn't truly begun to know the pileateds until the day I finally found their nest. Oblong cratered trees, chiseled by their great bills, were a familiar sight, and, like a bouquet of bloodroot in late April, their deep, loud drumming had been a dependable spring event; yet the birds themselves were still strangers to me. Even numerous sightings of these crow-sized woodpeckers, their white underwings flashing as they flew through the green wood or across the meadow, left me wanting more. I found their nest in early May and that made all the difference.

The woodpeckers led me to it as they cavorted about the woods, chasing one another from tree to tree until one of the birds suddenly vanished, apparently into a dead elm. This tree had been standing dead for many years; its upper branches and bark had long since fallen. Only the forked trunk remained erect, and as I moved closer to investigate, a female pileated poked her head from a neat round hole about eighteen feet above the

131

ground. The nest cavity faced Blood Brook to the south, so the sun moving across the sky would warm the tree and help incubate her round white eggs. The muffled call of her mate wafted by, but instead of answering, she followed the noise with her eyes, lowering and raising her red crest. Her white facial stripes reflected the midafternoon light as she peered across the forest, but when she finally withdrew into the nest chamber, the elm seemed as lifeless as before she had arrived.

I set up a green nylon observation blind, and for eighteen days watched the parent birds as they prepared for the arrival of their young. Unlike other North American woodpeckers, pileateds mate for life, and share the chores of warming and turning the eggs that lie nestled in wood chips in their lofty nest. Although the two birds took turns guarding the nest by day, the female departed each evening at twilight for a distant roost hole somewhere on Spaulding Hill, leaving the nest to her mate's care. At dawn she would reappear, and temporarily relieved of duty, the male would then depart into the awakening woods. Every hour or two throughout the day the birds exchanged positions until dark when the male resumed his vigil.

That was the most habitual pattern I ever noticed, although I've heard others assert that pileateds make regular stops during a day's foraging. In fact, a friend of mine who lives across the Connecticut River in Haverhill, New Hampshire, reports that several summers ago a lone pileated delighted townspeople for many weeks by visiting a dying roadside maple every Tuesday, Thursday, and Sunday at 1:00 P.M., give or take a little. The Blood Brook woodpeckers were never that precise, except in the male's nightly return at sundown to tend the eggs.

Ineffably delighted, I crouched in the blind at dawn, awaiting the return of the mother pileated. The air was thick and redolent with brambles, which grow in profusion in the clearing adjacent to our meadow, and the brook's lilt muffled the sweet but monotonous phrases of a red-eyed vireo. As the morning warmed, fog dispersed and mosquitoes began to whine and bite; I slapped, pinched, flicked, and squeezed them, until I was forced to hold them at bay with reams of blue cigar smoke. Alternatingly lulled by the ambiance of birdsong and preoccupied by mosquitoes, I waited. When the female pileated finally arrived, for a moment I held my breath. She regarded the blind with indifference, hit the elm with a thud, then climbed directly to the cavity, her tail pressed against the trunk and her back parallel to it.

To the Western Abenaki, the pileated was *Pachpaskaissi*, a word that when pronounced slowly, accenting the *p*'s and the *k*'s as though pounding a hammer, has an onomatopoetic ring and means "pounding his nose." Although this bird has sported numerous colorful names—cock-of-the-woods, king-of-the-woods, Indian-hen, stump-breaker, laughing woodpecker, cluck-cock, and Lord-God-bird—log-cock was the most widely used name. Mark Catesby, the eighteenth-century naturalist who wrote *The Natural History of Carolina, Florida, and the Bahama Islands*, called the pileated the large red-crested woodpecker. When Carl von Linnaeus, the father of the binomial system for scientific nomenclature, sought a Latin name for Catesby's bird, he called it *Dryocopus pileatus*, which means crested tree-cleaver. Eventually, von Linnaeus's weighty name for the woodpecker was clipped and anglicized to pileated. Unfortunately, lamented Arthur Cleveland Bent, author of the landmark twenty-six-volume *Life History of North American Birds*, "the bird already possessed a common name [log cock] and it is a pity that [they] did not know it. . . . And now upon this splendid creature a dull piece of pedantry remains hopelessly fixed."

By late May the birds had hatched. Their presence was indicated by a peculiar buzzing sound, more typical of a swarm of hornets or a congregation of bees. The elm seemed to vibrate with the noise. Lawrence Kilham, New England's most inveterate woodpecker watcher and author of On Watching Birds, suspects that these odd guttural buzzes made by the infant woodpeckers may serve to discourage raiding squirrels or raccoons, for what nest robber would choose to tangle with so many angry stinging insects? Once, I placed my ear against the trunk and listened to the tree resonate, a sound that I assume moved from the elm to the ground and sent ripples through the earth like a vibrating tuning fork touching water. I wondered if worms and moles heard—or felt—the low-frequency serenade, the faint sound waves that radiated out from the base of the elm. The more the tree purred, the more I imagined.

Although the young woodpeckers were unable to reach the mouth of their cavity, about twelve inches above the floor, they knew when a parent drew near; their mumblings increased to an alarming volume each time a pileated swung past my view. Pandemonium broke loose as an adult reached the elm and began its vertical ascent to the nest hole. Tilting downward into the chamber, arching its stiff black tail feathers against the ceiling of the cavity, the parent would enter the nest, quivering violently as regurgitated ants, beetle larvae, and caterpillars slid down the throats of its anxious brood.

After each feeding the adult would disappear into the nest chamber for a minute or two and slowly emerge with its mouth crammed with membranous packets of feces, each twisted at the end, then inconspicuously slip into the woods to deposit the packets some distance from the nest. This procedure, which was faithfully performed, kept the nest and its young occupants clean and helped to eliminate odors that might lure hungry predators.

Before the era of market hunting, the golden age of wildlife slaughter when even the pileated was sold as food, wildlife was not so shy. Many species of mammals that are now nocturnal foraged in daylight, some even walked in the shadow of humans. More than two hundred years of persecution have increased most animals' flight distance—inviolable space that an animal keeps between itself and another species. Slowly walk toward your bird feeder. How close can you get before the blue jay or chickadee flies? That's flight distance.

Flight distance is a window into an animal's personality, an indicator of its sense of security. Fast animals such as snowshoe hares have shorter flight distances than slower animals like woodchucks, and powerful animals have shorter flight distances than meek animals: moose are easier to approach than deer. Aquatic animals have shorter flight distances in water than on land; try to approach a beaver on land. Because of their camouflage, grouse have very short flight distances. For the pileated, as with most animals, flight distance also varies according to the species encountered: a goshawk ripping into the woods provokes an immediate exodus, but a white-breasted nuthatch foraging on the same trunk may be ignored by the woodpecker. Caribou graze near wolves that are at rest or at play, but if the wolves put their noses to the ground and press back their ears, caribou run.

Young animals usually have shorter flight distances than their parents. Depending on your point of view, the reluctance of a young animal to flee is either an example of blind innocence or a vestigial ignorance—in either case, the pup or fawn or kit or fledgling has not yet learned to fear people.

Several months ago, while I was photographing a California black oak frosted with rime ice in Yosemite National Park, a coyote passed through my frame, within fifty yards of me, glanced obliquely my way, then walked away. Yet here along Blood Brook, coyotes slink in the shadows or hunt the far side of the meadow, well away from passers-by.

Whenever I find a wild mammal or bird along Blood Brook which permits a closer than usual approach as it goes about its daily business, I consider the event a gift. When I first found the pileated nest, I squatted like a fugitive in the blind, twenty feet away. Slowly I moved the blind closer, a few feet a day, until I crouched five feet from the elm. By the end of the second week of incubation, I sat in a lawn chair outside the blind, notebook and pencil in hand, in full view of the birds, which had accepted me. Eventually, I set up more chairs and so had elm-side company for lunch, libations, and woodpecker watching.

By the time the chicks were a week old, I could stand on the penultimate rung of a homemade wooden ladder, which leaned against an adjacent pine, camera in hand, strobe lights bungied to another neighboring tree, only five feet from the nest cavity.

The young woodpeckers grew quickly, nourished by the copious harvest of insects provided by the adult birds, whose ability to detect carpenter ants was uncanny. Although early naturalists believed the strong formic acid smell of the ants attracted the woodpeckers, Kilham suggests that a visual clue—perhaps a shelf fungus or a canker—attracts the pileated to an ant tree. It also seems likely that woodpeckers utilize sound. Repeated soundings along the side of the trunk, like those made by a prudent shopper testing a watermelon, would disclose the ant colony. However the detection is accomplished, I could see as I wandered through the valley that the heartwood of every stump and trunk the pileateds had chiseled with their powerful bills was laced with ant tunnels. Huge rectangular excavations more than a foot long, four or five inches wide, and as many inches deep laid bare the ant galleries. The adults returned to the ravaged ant trees fifteen or twenty times each day. After harvesting the ants with their long sticky tongues, they returned to the nest to feed their young.

I saw the little woodpeckers for the first time during the second week in June. At that time two males, whose red crests extend to their upper bills, and a female, whose red crest stops at eye level, began poking their heads into the outside world, incessantly mimicking the calls of their parents. I watched as the adults, back from foraging excursions, strategically positioned themselves behind a large white pine. Hopping in and out of view, they tried to assess my intentions before moving to the nest. The screaming young birds jostled one another, nearly falling from the elm as they waited for their mother or father to thrust food deep into their throats.

For these birds, the nesting season was progressing smoothly, but food and nesting places have not always been so plentiful for the pileateds, the largest of nineteen species of woodpeckers native to this continent, now that the larger and whiter ivory-billed woodpecker of southern bottomland forests is extinct in North America. (A small population of ivorybills still bangs away in Cuban pinelands.) The pileated's domain once extended, unbroken, from northern British Columbia to Nova Scotia and from central California to southern Florida, but as forests shrunk to woodlots, pileateds, like the ivorybills, disappeared from the countryside. By the nineteenth century, when most of the deciduous forest in the Northeast has been divided into farms and pastures, the big woodpeckers were scarce. Thoreau never saw one, and John Burroughs, whose nature essays were extremely popular around the turn of the century, never heard one.

Fortunately for the pileateds, land-use practices shifted. The abandonment of farms and the subsequent reforestation of fields meant that new homes and food sources were available, and the woodpecker population began to increase. As meadows became crowded with pine and maple, and pastoral landscapes reverted to second-growth woods, more and more pileateds returned. Dutch elm disease offered the birds a pantry of carpenter ants and beetles, as well as numerous potential nesting sites. Once again, in early March, the woodpeckers' resonant drumming has become a familiar sound, reverberating from dawn to dusk across much of their former range.

This drumming—its numerous powerful blows lasting several seconds, then quieting near the end of each roll—is perhaps the most familiar characteristic of the pileateds, and I noticed that the young birds instinctively began practicing their drumming soon after they had hatched. Muted though the sound was, the frequency and rhythm of their efforts were much like those of their parents, who by this time of the year had nearly ceased their own pounding; ant-filled feeding trees are softer, often punky, and far less musical than drumming trees. The young persisted, even without their parents' example. The pileateds' drumming serves several purposes: to announce territorial ownership, to attract a would-be mate, or to call a mate. Eventually the drumming of the young woodpeckers I watched would resonate from the dead limbs and hollow trees of Blood Brook valley, even from the metal roofs of houses and barns, much to the annoyance of the human occupants, but for now the young birds were content to tap their bills on the walls of the nest chamber.

By the third week of June the nearly full-grown young were perched precariously on the rim of the nest hole, filling the opening. Heralding their first flight, the parents began a duet that filled the forest with loud, derisive laughter, like cries of the deeply disturbed. All afternoon the parent birds summoned, while the young birds listened and watched, gathering courage to jump, like kids preparing to enter a cool lake. Lured by the relentless *cuk*-ing calls of their parents, the young birds leaned toward the beckoning forest, and on the morning of the summer solstice the first two birds took flight. The third followed the next day.

During the next several weeks I could see the young in the vicinity of the elm, fluttering through the woods and across the meadow as they plaintively begged for food. Their parents faithfully tended to their needs, leading them to ants, teaching them the art of finding beetle larvae under tussocks of moss, and instructing them in the proper techniques of eviscerating the rotting stumps on the slope above the driveway. Once, two young woodpeckers and a parent, like a tercet of pterodactyls, crossed the meadow below Blood Brook, their stiff wings flashing white, crests backlit and flaming. They flew into the front yard maple, and perched on the trunk in view of the window, squabbling and chasing, then disappeared into the woods on the west side of the house.

With time the young birds became more independent. By autumn their apprenticeship was over, and they traveled unescorted to the wild arbors of grape. As the days grew shorter and colder the pileated began consuming quantities of clustered dogwood fruits, racemes of cherry, and poison ivy berries, eating their fill before the hordes of migratory birds could strip the woods bare of its remaining fruits.

Watching their autumnal foraging was hilarious, for pileateds eating fruit are a comic sight. They would grasp the spindly branches and hang upside down, parrotlike, screaming wildly as though in distress and consuming one piece at a time. Kilham believes the birds are vulnerable in these positions, and that their excited cries are a ploy to deter potential predators—goshawks, Cooper's hawks, peregrine falcons, or, if they forage near the ground, bobcats, fishers, coyotes, and foxes. Humans too, were once a predator of the woodpecker. The Huron Indians adorned their calumets with pileated crest feathers and made necklaces from their huge bills. At one time the birds were even sold in the markets of large eastern cities, but Audubon found the meat tough and smelly, and Major Charles Bendire, writing in 1895 about birds for the U.S. National Museum (the precursor of the Smithsonian Institution) found pileateds "a very unpalatable substitute for game of any kind," despite "any amount of seasoning and cooking."

Although market hunting no longer endangers the species, rapid deforestation again threatens the pileateds' food supply and nesting sites. As my neighbors remove standing dead timber, the young woodpeckers find the resources critical to their survival growing scarcer. Some foresters and recreation managers are well aware of the threat. The U.S. Forest Service has established a policy in western national forests that requires loggers "to provide habitat needed to maintain viable populations of cavity-nesting wildlife." To the chagrin of some woodcutters, the Forest Service advocates that selected trees which might otherwise be taken for firewood be left standing for cavity nesters. My neighbors, I hope, will understand, and thin their woods selectively, leaving a few trees per acre for the pileateds, especially dead elms.

For as winter approaches, each of the woodpeckers must find a separate roost hole to shelter it from the prevailing winds. The pileated has no need to migrate, because its principal food supply is well insulated and accessible all winter. The male I had been observing appropriated the old nest hole, returning each evening alone, while his mate excavated another hole about a half-mile away. The young birds had to travel, for not only did they need roost holes, they also had to find territories that would supply them with food. They were no longer tolerated in the valley, and at times they were driven from the neighborhood by their parents.

All these additional winter roost holes, and new nest holes every spring, ultimately provide many woodland creatures with shelter. I've noticed a saw-whet owl inspecting an old pileated nest cavity, and squirrels, too, rely to some extent on these energetic woodpeckers to provide new dwellings.

By next March, in a cranny of Blood Brook valley, a young pileated will sound its drum, only barely audible from our house. Perhaps it will be calling a mate it has never met or merely answering the echoes of its parents. I will search for the nest, for proximity to wildlife is an elixir: a chance to sit still and watch, to while away the hours in the name of natural science, to lose myself again. For me, watching wildlife is what Ponce de León searched in vain for, a fountain of youth.

A Neighborly
Whippoorwill

Whippoorwills usher dusk through the north end of our valley. In July, they begin calling by 8:45 P.M., in September by 7:00 P.M.; both times they continue for more than an hour before stopping. Then, an hour before dawn moves in over Bald Top, their serenade resumes until sunrise. On bright, moonlit nights they sing without pause, wild, forlorn cries rebounding out of the summer twilight with hypnotic force. Hearing them, I am a boy again at summer camp in East Wolfboro, New Hampshire, walking in woods behind my cabin; or I am scuffing through Long Island's Pine Barrens, where a dozen whistled in the moonlight.

One evening several days after the full moon in June, I left an outside light on while I worked in the studio. Lured by the radiance, scores of moths gathered above the deck, drunk on porch light. Lured by the moths, a whippoorwill settled nearby and jarred the night with loud, incessant calls. I listened intently, then slid the studio door open. With ruby eyes that glowed like embers, the bird perched lengthwise on a thick, horizontal branch of the white ash, and called his name forty-seven times in less than a minute, accenting the first and last syllables, and ending each call with a soft cluck. With each call, his throat slightly swelled, which made his white necklace blink in the lamp light. Slowly, I crossed the deck—twenty, fifteen, ten feet away. The whippoorwill left his perch, fluttered mothlike above the lawn, white-tipped tail feathers fanning and mouth gaping. A moth disappeared. Back in the ash, he fired eighty-six staccato cries, then left to chase another moth.

When I turned the porch light off, the moths dispersed, the whippoorwill vanished, and the night lost eloquence.

There is a certain level of familiarity, or so I thought, which I have been acquiring for the meadows and woods that stretch from my doorstep. I have worn a path down to the brook, through the maples and pines, around the tiny cattail marsh at the northeast corner of the pond. I have explored Bald Top, all the dips and undulations in our meadow, and I have walked the face of Spaulding Hill from Brushwood Road to the beaver pond that drains toward Lake Morey. Blood Brook valley has been the site of numerous rambles; yet at four in the morning, as I paused in the meadow south of our house, my neighborhood dissolved into shadows and silver light. There was a deep blue hush to the predawn, a sense of mystery and adventure in an undiscovered valley. Spread before me was a land once known, but now barely recognized.

Grass curved with dew. Mist rose from the pond and brook, while distant mounds of fog coalesced above Lake Fairlee and accumulated in the valley. Green frogs twanged, like a summer metronome. In the pines below our meadow, two whippoorwills argued in the dim light, a father and son, perhaps, establishing boundaries. Are we much different than birds? I cupped my hands around my ears to amplify their dispute. As the sky gradually lightened, I followed the brook toward the whippoorwills.

The woods roiled with an emphatic duet. How could the pileated woodpeckers or any creature not deaf still be asleep? The whippoorwills called and called and called. These are birds from the boundaries of night, whose crepuscular cries overlap the hours of both owls and thrushes.

Over and over the whippoorwills repeat their names—*whip-poor-will, whip-poor-will*—barely pausing for breath. I find it hard to believe that birds can be so persistent, but nearly ninety years ago John Burroughs, writing about his native Catskill Mountains, counted 1088 consecutive calls. John Hay, who has written often and eloquently about Cape Cod, once tallied 1136 calls before falling asleep with the whippoorwill still calling. Those are both impressive records, though I am not sure who deserves more credit for endurance, the whippoorwills or Burroughs and Hay. Blood Brook's males have record potential.

After five minutes of acoustic warfare, the whippoorwills negotiated a truce and disbanded. One called from out of the mist beyond our pond. An answer descended from Bald Top. I left the woods and walked to the road. The wedge-shaped hind wing of a polyphemus moth rested on the shoulder of Bloodbrook Road; the wing's round eyespot, bright yellow surrounded by purple and black, suggested an owl eye, perhaps, a saw-whet or an eastern screech. Like woodcutters along the Ganges delta who wear face masks on the back of their heads to confuse Bengal tigers, which only attack from the back, polyphemus moths have eyespots on their wings to fool would-be predators into thinking they face an angry, alert owl.

Whippoorwills relish these big, juicy *saturniid* moths. After their June metamorphosis, polyphemus moths (as well as the even larger luna and cecropia moths), whose only ambitions are to mate, perfume the night wind with pheromones. Whippoorwills are so often associated with these mammoth moths that Audubon painted a whippoorwill with an Ethel Merman mouth pursuing a cecropia, a moth as big as an oak leaf, with several square inches of soft, protein-rich abdomen.

All summer long, whippoorwills troll for insects from the big red oaks near Brushwood Road, where Bloodbrook Road angles sharply west, south above a half-mile of variegated woods and meadows. Their activities bind four properties—Floryan, Neilson-Rinaldo, Levin, Monteith—into a single, heterogeneous whippoorwill territory, replete with singing posts and moth-attracting porch lights.

Unlike dooryard phoebes and bluebirds, which confine their activities to the vicinity of our house, rarely crossing a property line, and unlike the sharp-shinned hawks, which nest on Spaulding Hill and patrol the upper drainage of both Blood Brook and Middle Brook from Bald Top west to Wild Hill, the whippoorwills are neighborly and visit all four families every night, calling from virtually the same limbs and rocks and rooftops night after night throughout the summer.

I suspect that the whippoorwills incubate in pine-shade below our southern boundary, where the June males had engaged in vociferous battle. Once territorial boundaries have been established, courtship begins, and almost every evening an hour after sunset, from late May through mid-September, a male begins calling from south of the stone wall that separates our meadow from the Monteiths. Then he either moves to our property, or bypasses us and flies to the Floryins' meadow, from where his voice is barely audible. Whenever the whippoorwill comes to us, his voice springs from either the sapling maples and stone wall on the west side of our meadow, or from the dead, pondside elm to the east. If the outside lights are on, he calls from the roof of our house, invariably waking us up.

Early one morning, several days after the summer solstice, I found a road-killed female whippoorwill past the turn-off for Brushwood Road, half a mile before our driveway. Extending vertically above a bed of brown leaves, one wing flagged me down. The carcass was cool and soft; the bird had probably been struck by a car the previous night when she dipped across the road in pursuit of an insect. Unlike the moth-chasing male I had watched, this whippoorwill had a buff-colored necklace and lacked the white-tipped outer tail feathers. I took the bird home to show Casey the delicate colors and to introduce him to death.

This whippoorwill was the color of the forest floor on which she nested, brown vermiculated with gray, black, and buff. Her feathers were velvety owl-like. Her wings were short and rounded, her tail six inches long. Her mouth was enormous. A comb of stiff, bristly feathers extended beyond her small bill. Casey waited for the whippoorwill to come to life, to sit panting in my hand then fly away, like a stunned bird recuperating from a collision with our window.

I told Casey that the bird came from the earth and would return to it, like mountains that become plains, or lakes that become bogs then forests. To demonstrate the point, I placed the bird on a pine stump scaffold, and for several days we watched the earth take her back. That first morning, the whippoorwill swarmed with ants. By the second morning, orange and black carrion beetles and white maggots had dismantled her. Because she smelled putrid, the following day, Casey abandoned his post at the stump. A week later, eddies of down drifted across the garden. The wing and tail feathers and the greasy, articulated skeleton slipped off the stump and were eventually ground into the meadow.

Five months after the whippoorwill disintegrated, Linny's father died. The three of us flew to Fort Thomas, Kentucky, for the wake and funeral, which was, for the most part, a denial of natural cycles. Embalming was only the beginning. The cemetery staff had blanketed the waiting mound of earth and fringed the grave with Astro Turf. Once lowered, the coffin would rest on a panel of brown plastic. Linny encouraged Casey to reach in and push back the skirt of Astro Turf, to see unglaciated Kentucky soil, weathered stones, and twisted roots, to know that grandpa's cells might resurrect as a black-eyed Susan. Casey dropped a native black walnut and sprinkled a vial of Ohio River water into the grave: "Would grandpa feed the tree?"

One night last July, Chuck Eaton from Middle Brook, who had grown up listening to whippoorwills, came to our house hoping to hear a voice from his past. I chummed the whippoorwill with the outside lights, and we stood on the driveway listening to its distant, plaintive call. Then the bird stopped. Minutes later, three soft clucks wafted from the white ash next to my studio, followed by a salvo of five *whip*-poor-*wills*. Each *will* was followed by a single cluck. The bird had flown over the house, landing twenty feet from us. He bobbed and davened on the branch, then caught a moth above the lawn, snaring the insect like a flycatcher. Instead of returning to the ash, he veered east, disappearing into the darkness behind the pond. Several minutes later, a whippoorwill called from across the meadows, distant but poignant, like the memories of childhood.

The Last Rattlesnakes

Refugees from a warmer past, timber rattlesnakes probably slaked their thirst in Blood Brook, hibernated in the ledges of Spaulding Hill, and sounded their castanets to Paleolithic Indians, more than five thousand years ago. Change drives evolution and the earth itself is the vehicle: the planet spins, and day replaces night; rotates, and spring replaces winter. Continents stray. Climates oscillate. Species arise, fracture into races, spawn new species, or slowly stagnate and then die.

Vermont's present distribution of plants and animals is a mosaic, a fragmented record of the sweeping climactic changes since the recession of the last glacier. Between four and six thousand years ago, the Northeast basked in a climactic optimum, the hypsithermal interval. Winters were warmer and shorter, while summers were longer, hotter, and wetter then they are now. Without the sharp contrast between warm days and cool nights, fall color along Blood Brook must have been duller and the spring run of maple sap earlier, briefer, and not nearly as plentiful.

Like the arctic tundra communities before them, the biotic communities that characterized the hypsithermal interval retreated as the climate changed, leaving behind relics of their passing in warm, protected pockets of northern woodlands. Insectivorous plants and peatland orchids, which have rallied in bogs and fens, grow alongside arctic and boreal species, themselves relics of a cooler epoch. In Vermont, timber rattlesnakes live at the northernmost edge of distribution for the entire tribe and continue to roll evolution's dice, gambling that in a land with little competition they can survive and reproduce during an abbreviated growing season.

For a timber rattlesnake to prosper, the number of frost-free days is not nearly so important as the number of days the snake's body temperature is above seventy degrees Fahrenheit, the lower end of its optimal range of temperature. If timber rattlesnakes were classified like garden vegetables they would be Zone 4 natives, found in Zone 3. To carry this analogy one step further, if you wanted them in your yard, you would have to start them indoors under grow lights, transfer them to a cold frame on the first of May, then plant them sometime after Memorial Day. They would be harder to start than melons, slower growing than black walnuts, and, like September basil, need a blanket of newspapers at the first hint of frost.

A Methuselah timber rattlesnake may be more than thirty years old, more than three feet long, and as thick as my wrist— three or four times the girth of a milk snake of similar length. Yet rattlesnakes have the shortest growing season of Vermont's eleven species of snakes. Most rattlesnakes will not leave their ancestral dens (or hibernacula) among the talus and exfoliating ledges on southwest facing hills until early May. For a few weeks they loiter on the ledges soaking up spring sunshine and retreat-ing below the surface during night when the temperature drops; small rattlesnakes, with less heat-retaining mass, stick close to the den. When night temperatures rise to a comfortable level, many rattlesnakes leave the ledges for nearby wooded valleys.

By late August, they reconvene near the den. Some give birth. Others come to breed. All await the frost. As the nights grow pro-gressively longer and colder, they stop crawling to the surface of ledges to sun themselves and, instead, remain below the frost line at the base of deep vertical fissures, sometimes twenty or more feet below the ground, balled in serpentine knots. After eight months of hibernation, they reemerge. Hundreds of rattlesnakes once shared the same hibernaculum. When I visited New York State's Dutchess County dens, I was astonished to find the en-trances worn smooth by the abrasive action of belly scales: so many snakes for so many years had scoured the rock with the force of running water.

I imagine that last April's unseasonable warmth roused the Vermont rattlesnakes and that they gathered on warm ledges close to home, their dark bodies functioning in the sun like solar collectors. Some shed their skins. Some fed. Ninety degrees Fahrenheit in mid-April must have been ecstasy. When May fol-lowed, impersonating November, their world must have shattered. As their body temperatures dropped, their rates of metabolism would have slowed; a swallowed chipmunk would have sat undi-gested, a knot in the middle of a living rope.

On the Friday before Memorial Day, the sky turned blue and temperatures rose into the mid-seventies. I decided to search for rattlesnakes as they relaxed in the sun, to see a reflection of Blood Brook circa five thousand years ago, when Vermont proba-bly resembled present day Virginia. My destination was the ledges above the southern end of Lake Champlain, where the lake narrows to the width of a river, and Vermont's border, having run north from the Massachusetts line for fifty perfectly straight miles, doglegs toward New York.

The ledges face southwest, rise from the valley for several hundred feet, and, in addition to several snake dens, support a disjunct population of five-lined skinks. Vermont's only lizard, the skinks share a similar demography with the rattlesnakes: widely scattered colonies, vestiges from the prehistoric warm spell when both reptiles crept over much of the Northeast. A wet meadow stretching from the lake to the base of the bluffs marks the former flood plain of the Hudson River, which emptied Lake Champlain for several thousand years after the Ice Age. Champlain's long tail, which dominates the view from the top of the ledges, follows the Hudson's old drainage.

This is an isolated section of Vermont, a rural farming community cut off from the rest of the state by New York, which surrounds it on three sides; in fact, you can watch the sun rise over New York. To reach the timber rattlesnakes, I drove into New York then crossed back into Vermont on an unimproved, unmarked, beaver-flooded dirt road that sees more muskrats than cars.

Because this was my first trip to the site and because rattlesnakes are particular in their choice of dens, selecting a single crack in more than a quarter-mile of ledges, I needed an escort familiar with the area and the habits of rattlesnakes. My guide was Marc DesMeules, the director of Science and Stewardship for the Vermont Nature Conservancy. He knew the precise location of a den where rattlesnakes sunbathed and guaranteed me that I would see them, as though he were promising a look at rare plants rooted to a definite site rather than timid and secretive animals. In the Northeast, in fact, rattlesnakes and bog orchids have several traits in common; both moved north during the hypsithermal warming period, and both occur in widely scattered, small populations that are vulnerable to amateur collectors who lust for them because of their rarity.

Although I had never seen a rattlesnake in New England, I had seen them in the deserts of California and Arizona, on the High Plains of South Dakota, in the swamps of Georgia. One night in Pinto Basin in southeastern California, with the aid of an extended tripod leg, I shepherded nine rattlesnakes off the road. I know that for most people rattlesnakes symbolize a dark zone ruled by fear, the very worst nature has to offer.

Several years ago, National Public Radio's evening news program "All Things Considered" interviewed David Shepherd, a biologist at Southern Louisiana State University who had studied the response of motorists to the sight of a rubber snake or turtle in the road. Shepherd placed the toys on a highway, hid himself in nearby bushes, and watched cars pass. Of the 7600 motorists who approached the snake, 498 (or 1 out of 15) deviated from their path to hit it, almost double the number that deliberately struck the turtle.

Nearly twenty years ago, as I drove through Georgia's Okefenokee Swamp, an eastern diamondback eased onto the opposite side of the road. The diamondback is among the longest species of snake in North America, certainly the heaviest, and, because of its size and the amount of venom it produces, one of the world's deadliest. I stopped to watch. As the rattlesnake crossed the lanes, an ophidiophobic driver heading toward me cut to my side of the road, ran over the snake with an audible, sickening crunch, then swerved back into his own lane. Too injured to crawl or to coil in defense, the diamondback writhed on the hot pavement. The snake was a monster: more than six feet long and thick as an oak limb, with a wide triangular head the size of the palm of my hand and a thirteen-button rattle. I very carefully stole its skin, which still hangs in my office. In its stomach was a full-grown marsh rabbit.

Driving, I trailed Marc DesMeules past old farmhouses and barns, across Champlain's wet meadows, as mud splattered from our wheels. We drove until we could drive no further. The gray ledge, framed by the summer-green woods, rose from the meadow a half mile to our north. We waded through the ankle-high grasses, leopard frogs popping at our feet, and climbed an indistinct woodland trail that curled through a hickory forest.

Ravens circled the ledge. A turkey vulture and a red-tailed hawk soared past. A golden-winged warbler crooned from an elm branch. I had been searching for Vermont timber rattlesnakes for fifteen years, and the promise of finally seeing these orphans from a wilder, warmer, more remote Vermont, pulled me forward. I am still amazed that rattlesnakes live in Vermont. During the late spring and early fall, they bask all day, sleep all night. In summer they emerge at night to ambush warm-blooded prey, for instance mice that wander within their striking range, which is about half their body length. According to William S. Brown, Skidmore College biologist and rattlesnake researcher, a Northeast timber rattlesnake feeds only six to twenty times a year, mostly on white-footed mice and chipmunks, and grows so slowly that it does not reach sexual maturity until it is six to eight years old. Although these snakes have small litters, averaging nine young, the large embryos fill the female's body cavity, forcing her to stop feeding. Pregnancy so depletes her energy reserves that a female timber rattlesnake breeds only once every three years.

I followed Marc up the trail through moist bottom land into a dry, sparsely wooded, very stunted oak-hickory forest. A band of calf-high grasses studded with long, flat, rock slabs grows beneath the oaks and hickories and stretches around the belly of the hill like a frayed skirt. This was timber rattlesnake country, the

threshold of one of the region's most precious sanctums. I measured every step.

With the help of the Vermont Housing and Conservation
Trust Fund, the Nature Conservancy bought this 1500-acre
patchwork of farmland, wet meadows, woods, and mountain,
which includes the flaking snake ledges, in December 1989 for
$1.2 million, the Vermont chapter's most expensive land acquisi-
tion. The purchase took years of difficult fundraising. Some sup-
porters found the idea of using hard-won funds to save poisonous
snakes repulsive, an idea as insane as buying Ted Bundy a place at
a summer camp. To naturalists, however, the preservation of one
of Vermont's two known rattlesnake dens was a conservation
milestone, the result of a bold effort to protect a critically endangered species whose existence is threatened both by those who
hate it and those who covet its prize skin.

Vermont supported as many as thirty dens during the 1800s,
mostly in the Champlain Valley and Connecticut Valley: Shaw
Mountain, Snake Mountain, Arrowhead Mountain, Mount Independence, Little Ascutney, Glen Lake Cliffs, and Fifteen Mile Falls
all harbored snakes at one time. Until 1971 Vermont encouraged
the destruction of rattlesnakes by offering a dollar bounty for a
set of rattles brought to any town clerk. The bounty system and
the fear of rattlesnakes brought people to the ledges with rifles,
axes, and clubs. It is a wonder that any snakes survive.

Many historic sites have been worked so often by collectors
that the dens are now empty. The taking of timber rattlesnakes
for the now illegal live-animal trade by an illicit network of collectors, dealers, and buyers threatens to clean out the remaining
dens in the Northeast. Normally yellow, brown, or gray with unmarked heads and dark blotches that form cross bands on the
rear in southern and western portions of their range, some northern rattlesnakes are almost black. These melanistic specimens,

mostly males, bring a high price on the live-snake market and are sought by amateur snake fanciers for their private menageries.

I received a wildlife alert in the mail last summer from the New York State Department of Environmental Conservation, an alarming rattlesnake all points bulletin. The alert reported that Rudy Komarek, a notorious snake collector from southern New Jersey, intended to hunt northeastern timber rattlesnakes that summer. It described Komarek—white, muscular, five feet four inches tall, straight brown hair graying at the temples and balding on top, fifty-nine, wearing glasses—and his green 1975 Chevy Nova, adding that state and federal authorities have been trying to apprehend him for illegal animal dealing, and that he has a criminal record that includes attempted manslaughter using live rattlesnakes.

On that day in late May, besides Marc DesMeules and myself, three others rounded out our group: another Nature Conservancy biologist, a writer, and a photographer. Single file we hiked, Marc in the lead and me following directly after, about five feet behind in the suicide position, mine being the legs most likely to be struck by a snake startled by the person who passes first. Trekking through Vermont rattlesnake country is different than trekking through the desert where paths are clear and you can see ahead. In a hickory glade, grasses and blueberry bushes screen the ground. Only the innumerable flat-topped rocks are bare. And since rocks often shelter snakes, you must walk with considered steps.

Halfway up the hill, I heard a buzz, a high trill that sounded more like a cicada or a cricket than a rattlesnake. Still, the noise communicated directly to my feet, like an audible caution signal at a crosswalk. I froze. To my right, less than three feet away, was a small timber rattlesnake, its two-button rattle deliriously shaking. The snake was yellow with brown bands, about eighteen inches long and probably not more than two years old. Feeling the vibration of my footfalls, the snake had coiled and raised its head, forked tongue suspended in midflick to gather odors for the Jacobson's organ, a chemo-receptor on the roof of the mouth. Although its blood runs cold, a rattlesnake's tongue reveals its mood. A provoked snake flicks more; an excited snake yawns to flood its mouth with stimuli.

For the moment, the small timber rattlesnake seemed to have a split personality. While its tongue lazily arced up and out, slightly quivering, its tail vibrated so quickly that the rattles blurred. The light buzzing that resulted, barely audible from twenty feet, was absorbed by the May woods. The shaker muscle which drives the rattle contracts extremely fast, is highly resistant to fatigue, and metabolizes either oxygen or the carbohydrate glycogen. If this intensity of metabolic ability were to occur in human leg muscles, it would allow runners to sprint for miles. Although unrecognized by *Guinness Book of World Records*, an annoyed western diamondback of some local repute once rattled continuously for more than three hours.

In the Flint Hills of northeastern Kansas, where timber rattlesnakes still haunt the wooded limestone ledges and massasauga rattlers patrol the grassland, homesteaders in the 1850s claimed that snakes relayed their alarm from den to den until the hills trembled with the sound of millions of agitated rattlesnakes. Fearing the snakes' umbrage, the people supposedly have hid in tornado cellars. But snakes lack a middle ear cavity and hear only vibrations that are carried from the ground through the jawbones and ribs, so they are deaf even to the sound of their own rattling.

Rattlesnakes originated on the high plains of North America during the dawn of the Pliocene epoch between four and twelve million years ago, when the interior grasslands were crowded with ancient horses, camels, and numerous species of bison and pronghorn that moved together across the prairie. One theory holds that rattlesnakes, which evolved amid all those cloven hooves, developed loosely attached kertin rattles on the end of their tails to amplify the vibratory noise, to help them avoid being stepped on. The trick works. I've seen horses flinch when they hear a rattler hidden in tall grass. On a recent trip to southern Arizona, as I stalked less than two feet behind a squat, lumbering gila monster, a mound of red sandstone suddenly came alive beneath the lizard's feet. The snake went crazy, buzzing. The lizard never flinched. I straightened as though I'd touched an electric fence, and by the time I regained my composure, the gila monster was gone. But the tiger rattlesnake held its ground, poised to strike. The snake was enraged, and its rattling accompanied me down the hill, out across the desert flats, and into the car, before dissolving into the grind of the engine.

Standing near the timber rattlesnake, I am reminded that the buzz of rattlesnakes is more than a warning; it is an agent of natural selection among animals other than rattlesnakes. Several years ago, when I heard a rattle in a South Dakota prairie dog town, I expected to see a snake in the mouth of a burrow, escaping the summer sun. Instead, a burrowing owl flew off. So close is the sound of the owl to that of a rattlesnake that in the laboratory California ground squirrels, which easily distinguish between the sounds of large and small snakes, were deaf to the difference between a large snake and the defensive chatter of burrowing owl. Since no other species of owl makes such a sound, the voice of the ground-dwelling burrowing owl appears to be a rare example of acoustic mimicry, where the owl fools potential predators into thinking a rodent burrow is occupied by a large rattlesnake.

The Champlain timber rattlesnake and I have no such evolutionary entanglement. Gently, I poked a tripod leg toward the snake, and it unwound, tail blurring and buzzing. Back and forth it crawled along the rock, exposing first its tail, then its head, rattling all the while. After watching the snake for a few minutes, we moved on up the hill.

Suddenly, Marc announced a second snake, slightly larger and bolder than the first, lying in rock shade along our path. Yellow-colored, too. It sat perfectly still as we passed.

My steps became calculated, for off to my left were the fabled ledges, a sudden, sheer drop in the middle of the hickory glade. Although the den was less than thirty feet away, I could not see it, for it was hidden by shelves of crumbling rocks. I hiked on, attended by thoughts of half-hidden rattlers lounging in rock shadows. Roots became snakes. Several times I reminded myself that rattlesnakes don't always rattle before striking, that their bite, a sudden sting, would feel like the snap of a branch against the calf, and that too much talking made you less alert, dulling the senses.

After a slow climb, we reached the top of Bald Mountain. The view from the summit is gorgeous: emerald green flatlands, waves of distant hills rolling westward with the sun. Three large, dark-colored snakes, almost black, lay motionless on the summit. Two were entwined under a rock awning: one had lost an eye, perhaps pecked out by a bird; the other rested in the open, rattle up, its vertically slit pupils trained on my movement. I knelt and alternately watched and photographed the exposed snake, a species whose company I had sought for many years, an animal familiar to less than twenty people in the entire state.

Moonless nights hobble me. Darkness steals my peripheral vision, as woods and glades fade to shades of gray, robbed of all detail as in an under-exposed photograph. My steps become tentative as I feel my way along forest paths, trying to resolve the night into a few ordered, manageable parts.

A friend once introduced me to a government catalog that sold army surplus items. For about a thousand dollars, I could buy a pair of infrared binoculars to perceive the infrared radiation emitted from warm objects, including people and other warm-blooded animals. With infrared binoculars, I could see in the night with the acuity of a rattlesnake.

The prominent facial pits of a rattlesnake, a pair of deep cavities on the side of the face below the eyes, function like a pinhole camera. Infrared radiation emitted from warm-blooded animals passes into the pit and strikes a less than paper-thin membrane (not even one-fourth the thickness of this page). Suspended in air and insulated from the snake's own body heat, the membrane stretches across the back of the pit and is filled with about seven thousand bushy, infrared-sensitive nerve endings. Each nerve ending excites a nerve cell, which transmits a message along a pair of nerve branches to the rattlesnake's hind brain, while simultaneous impulses travel to the portion of the midbrain that receives visual stimuli. In other words, visual and infrared images are overlaid and integrated in the brain and are simultaneously interpreted by the rattlesnake. The pits are sensitive only to moving objects, leaving the snake "blind" to the infrared heat that radiates from a sun-warmed rock, for instance. Or a still person.

Since the diameter of the pit opening is one-third the diameter of the heat-sensitive membrane, heat from a mouse strikes only a small portion of the membrane, enabling the snake to locate its source. A timber rattlesnake often lies hidden in the shadows along the edge of a fallen log, waiting for busy woodland mice. It carefully selects a log rich in rodent odors, perhaps checking several logs until the right one is found. There it may wait for hours, lower jaw pressed against the side of the log, scanning the length of the log with its eyes and pits. When a white-footed mouse scurries across the log, the rattlesnake feels the vibration in its jaw, then traces the animal's movement with both its eyes and infrared receptors. If the mouse passes within range, the snake strikes.

For a thousand dollars I could open up the night, see by infrared. For a thousand dollars I could receive "within five working days" what took the rattlesnake two million years of evolution to develop.

What kind of person could deliberately destroy a timber rattlesnake, emissary from another epoch whose reality I am only beginning to grasp?

Marc jarred me back into this world. "Ted, you're kneeling on fragrant sumac, another Vermont endangered species." So I was.

Death and Expectation

I grew up watching Walt Disney's true-life adventures, where exotic animals from exotic lands paraded across a suburban movie screen for hour after uninterrupted hour. Music woven through Disney's footage set a mood, a pace, often at the expense of reality. Remember the square-dancing tarantulas in "The Living Desert"? A foot-stomping fiddle run overlaid what was probably a life or death struggle between two female spiders, converting them into gay, quixotic figurants, blithe beyond belief.

Now middle-aged and far more cynical, I want the Disney spider scene directed with a Mel Brooks flare; I would have a camera pan from the "dancers" to the fiddlers, who play under the full press of the desert sun, like the black-tie orchestra in *Blazing Saddles*, stranded and performing in a bleacher in the middle of nowhere as one cowpoke chases another past them.

Remember the wild run of lemmings that leaped headlong from ledges into the unforgiving Arctic Ocean in Disney's *Arctic*

Wonderland? Ten years ago, while photographing the west coast of Hudson Bay, I met a wildlife cinematographer who, as a teen, had been hired by Walt Disney Productions to throw buckets of brown lemmings in front of the cameras during the production of *Arctic Wonderland,* to give the impression of overwhelming numbers. Disney wanted footage to corroborate the notion that the capricious, anomalous, egregious behavior of these rodents was a mass suicidal run to the sea. In fact, this legend was fabricated from the migrations of a related Scandinavian species.

One summer I found a honeybee apparently sipping nectar from a boneset that grew in the meadow in front of the house. Her long, tubular tongue extended like a New Year's party favor into one of the many quarter-inch white blossoms. Pollen dusted her legs. I stepped up to the flower and bent down so that my eyes were in line with the bee's. The bee, however, remained curiously still, as though suspended from the flower. I looked a little closer.

She was propped up from below the flower by the piercing and sucking mouthparts of two ambush bugs, one fixed to her throat, the other to her abdomen. No more than half an inch long, they bushwhack insects many times their own size.

An ambush bug selects a cluster of flowers, settles in, and waits for butterflies, bees, and wasps to make their rounds. This boneset hosted light-colored ambush bugs, white and yellow with a hint of green, perfectly camouflaged. Later in August, yellow-brown ambush bugs gather on goldenrod blossoms.

Slow-moving predators, ambush bugs have modified forelegs that serve as powerful grasping organs. Their tibia, the distal joint of the foreleg, is a small curved blade like a miniature scythe which snaps back into a groove on the short, thickened femur. Both tibia are armed with teeth. The entire leg looks like Popeye's arm—thin on either end, swollen in the middle.

When a bee lands near an ambush bug, the bug grabs it by any available body part: tongue, foot, antenna, or wing. Locked on, it probes the angry, thrashing bee, finds a soft spot, usually between the head and thorax or along the abdomen, and then inserts its hollow beak, pumping digestive enzymes that slowly make soup of the bee's innards. When the ambush bug is through feeding, all that is left of its victim is a dried husk.

As I watched the ambush bugs drain the honeybee, three parasitic flies, smaller than blackflies, settled on the bee's abdomen. They came for a free lunch. When the flies were done, they lumbered off, their transparent bellies swollen with bee juice. Twenty minutes later, the ambush bugs, too, were sated. They disappeared back into the cluster of flowers.

I had approached some flowers in my meadow as many of us approach nature itself, expecting a benign and beautiful true-life adventure: "Pollination in a Wet Meadow." Instead of a thirsty pollinator sipping nectar, I found a hapless cadaver. The adventure was true to life, and beautiful in its own way, but the script was by Poe, not Disney. Like the bee, I had been ambushed by my expectations.

Nature documentaries now come into our homes nightly, simultaneously educating us about animals and detaching us from the natural world. Rare wildlife, from remote corners of the globe, swirl across our screens, like nightly baseball highlights, tightly edited for maximum, sustained action. Packaged for the short attention span of the average television viewer, nature appears to be colorful, mysterious, dramatic, sometimes gruesome, and accessible to the point of promiscuity. Where are the clouds, the rain, the bone-chilling wind, the mosquitoes, the empty landscapes?

We marvel at films that take years to produce, then turn off the set and expect wild animals, with little effort on our part, to pour from the hills and valleys as though marching to Noah. A segment of "Wild America" showed an elk carcass that was visited in succession by a grizzly bear, a mountain lion, a wolf, and a wolverine, all in about five minutes. In part because we see wildlife dramatized on television so often, real nature bores us, since like a game of baseball nature is slow, unpredictable, and not shackled by time. One of the most important attributes of a nature guide (like that of a good baseball announcer) is to thread meaning and information into the lulls, which are often numerous and long, without being gratuitous. To vindicate nature and entertain the patrons on a whale watch without a whale, or a hawk watch without a hawk, tests the fiber of even the most experienced naturalist.

One winter, on tour with a group in the Florida Everglades, mosquitoes ravaged our camp, a rare winter occurrence. Expedited by ten inches of rain in January, spring came early. Pink calopogon flowered in the sawgrass; here and there, a wispy green cypress entertained a red and yellow- and purple-flowered bromeliad, like a corsage pinned to a lapel. Miles of brown sawgrass began to green, while box turtles and rattlesnakes moved to higher ground. Backlit orange ground fog softened the morning sun. On a short excursion down the Christian Point Trail to Florida Bay, we saw a low-tide feeding frenzy featuring fifteen or twenty species of birds, including a bald eagle, several ospreys, and reddish egrets. Yet despite these extraordinary encounters, most of our guests, who were eager, interested, knowledgeable amateur naturalists, could speak only of the mosquitoes that were after all also a byproduct of the early rain. For our guests, the insects of Christian Point had been a curse, a pox on the entire trip.

Back home, Linny and Casey caught a dusky salamander and a two-lined salamander in the shoals, a mile before Blood Brook reaches Lake Fairlee, two animals that would probably be overlooked in the filming of a Blood Brook wildlife documentary. And yet for the four-year-old child who stood in the brook turning over slippery green rocks and who caught the salamanders, the episode was rich with meaning. If Linny and Casey had watched a television documentary about salamanders instead of looking for them ankle deep in rushing water, would Casey's memory have been inscribed with the event? Not even the finest films in the world, can replace what actually happens to us.

During an advertisement on cable television for a Time/Life video about predation that showed a killer whale with its teeth clamped on a sea lion pup, the narrator boomed, "See why they're called animals." Gory and spectacular, the clip pandered to blood lust rather than to a consciousness of life and death.

On a bitter February morning on Bald Top, I found the messy remains of a snowshoe hare that had been waylaid by a bobcat. The cat had apparently crouched behind a log that lay across a well-worn hare trail. An icy oval depression held a few bobcat hairs where the animal had hunched, waiting. A hare had passed. The cat had sprung, bounded a few steps, then taken the hare apart.

Along Blood Brook, in the hemlocks just below my neighbor's pasture, where the view closes in to an intimate, compelling tableau of forest and ledge, I found a pile of grouse remains: beautiful tail feathers, primary and secondary wing feathers, and small, soft, mottled brown and white and gray contour feathers that overlap like shingles down the bird's back to hold out the rain.

Hit from behind by a goshawk while it fed, the grouse must have died without a struggle. No blood, just feathers and the buds of sweet gale littered the snow. Well-built for maneuvering around trees and branches, the long-tailed, short-winged goshawk is a powerful, agile predator with flame-colored eyes, a black cap, blue-gray back, and a cream-white belly. Larger than a crow, a wandering goshawk (or two) plays pirate in the valley for at least a few days every winter. Sometimes it catches a mourning dove at our feeder, sometimes a blue jay perched and calling in the open.

Near the grouse feathers, I saw a single line of bird tracks (four toes to a print, each ending in the clear, hooked mark of a sharp talon) and a deep trough where the grouse, firmly fixed in the hawk's foot, had been dragged through the snow. On either side of that, the hopping goshawk had left a series of parallel lines as it pushed forward on extended wing tips, like a skier using poles. One leg up, one leg down, pressing with the strength of its wings, the goshawk had hobbled with its prize to the brook.

Along the brook, at the base of a large hemlock, the goshawk finished plucking. Feathers were everywhere, and a little pile of undigested buds and needles, the victim's last supper, lay in the snow.

Apparently, the hawk had emptied the grouse's crop before disappearing into the woods to eat its own meal of the body.

A frozen deer carcass is one of the finest collectors of New England wildlife, particularly when the winter is fierce.

After the first deep snow, the white-tailed deer that have been dispersed across their summer range gather for the winter on hills with a southern exposure, and plenty of hemlock for browsing and holding back the snow. Because weakened deer die each winter, deer yards invite the attention of predators: Eastern coyotes, bobcats, fishers, and red and gray foxes routinely search deer yards for winter-killed deer. In spring, black bears come to gorge on the thawing remains.

In March, just before giving birth to three or four blind, help-less kits, a female fisher must find a large, dependable source of protein—for example, a deer carcass. So important is this protein bonanza, believes one researcher, that in the nearby White Mountains of New Hampshire, whose snow-capped rim I see from Bald Top, female fishers seek high-elevation deer yards for their den sites, to be near rut-weakened bucks who frequently succumb to harsh conditions.

Last winter, a south-bound bald eagle found a rock-hard deer on river ice just south of Lake Fairlee. After feeding for two mornings, the eagle left. A raven arrived, then more ravens, with a volley of *quorks*, and they stripped the deer, piece by frozen piece, scavenging all but the hide and the bones. Bernd Heinrich's book, *Ravens in Winter*, underscores the importance of carrion for juvenile ravens, whose gregarious nature evolved as a means of defending winter carcasses from territorial adults.

Shortly after I finished reading Heinrich's book, our local landfill was closed by the state for souring the East Branch of the Ompompanoosuc River, leaving conservation officer Evan Eastman without a burial ground for road-killed deer. Excited about the prospect of attracting ravens to our yard, I called Evan and asked for a couple of twisted, frozen carcasses. He was delighted to have a new repository, for landowners often complain about an "unsightly" carcass on their property, particularly if it is visible from a cross-country ski trail. I lugged the deer downhill to our pond and laid them alongside the dead elm. Chickadees and nuthatches took to the carcasses as if they were suet bags, stippling the flesh with their pointy bills. Hungry crows fed, then hid dollops of frozen flesh in the crowns of hardwoods, flying from deer to woods and back, all morning, every morning, until the bones were stripped of meat. Eventually, six weeks and four carcasses later, a pair of ravens came. And, in March, we had turkey vultures.

Death shadows us all. More than 95 percent of all the species of plants and animals that have ever lived on Earth have become extinct. Like individuals, species have life spans; species that live in stable habitats, such as tropical sea clams, tend to evolve more slowly than terrestrial species that constantly face change. A new species flourishes, matures, often dividing into subspecies (or races), which either evolve into new species or grow older, more conservative, ceasing to be adaptable, and ultimately disappearing when they can no longer change in response to change. California condors, vultures, which for tens of thousands of years roamed the skies from the Pacific Coast to Florida looking for carcasses of extinct Ice Age mammals, can no longer exist in the wild. Millions of dollars have been spent on a condor-breeding regime at the Los Angeles Zoo, so condors may again volplane over California—maybe even over the Grand Canyon, where they've been absent for several thousand years—returning to the "wild" as wards of the state, fully dependent on people for food. What will birds that once dined for weeks on a single rotting five-thousand-pound sloth eat? Road-killed ground squirrels? Jackrabbits? Even dead deer may be too small to suit them. The range of California condors has been shrinking, their population dwindling, since the Pleistocene ended. Even the carcasses of all the excess suburban deer in the Northeast would not support a prospering population of California condors.

Let them die with dignity. Their niche in North America now belongs to turkey vultures, which soar above Bald Top and across Blood Brook, descending to eat from the deer carcass I procured for them. Perhaps they're the prototype for a future evolutionary radiation, from which new species will descend.

Przewalski horses and Père David's deer live only in zoos. Released condors would join them, birds on life-support systems. All North America would be reduced to a zoo: far more beautiful and diverse than the Bronx or the San Diego zoos, but a zoo nevertheless, where everything is under control. Money delegated to condor recovery should buy critical habitat that serves a community of wildlife, a wetland or an old-growth forest.

In any case, we won't have to go to California to see the condor; if we wait a while, there will surely be a television documentary.

Several months ago, Omni published one of my transparencies, an image of a pert Connecticut River leopard frog, green with rows of black spots. It was printed small in the magazine, barely larger than a postage stamp and without surrounding habitat, as though it were a picture of a frog floating in space instead of squatting in a wet meadow. And the photo was situated in the "Continuum" section at the bottom right-hand corner of page 40 beneath a short article titled, "A Cruel Cut." The article alerted readers to a Dissection Hotline, 1-800-922-FROG, which offers counseling to students who refuse to pith, to cut, to peel, to slice, to probe the inside of a frog, often while its heart still beats.

Curious, I telephoned the hotline. A kindly voice with a Southern drawl answered my query and suggested computer simulation as an alternative to the scalpel. With "Operation Frog" or "Visifrog," I could dissect and reconstruct a frog, even view organs in detail with high-resolution graphics, all without getting my fingers greasy. She also recommended the book 67 *Ways to Save the Animals*, which I bought. When it arrived, I turned to the section titled "Classroom Dissection: You Don't Have to Do It," and read that every year nearly six million animals—mostly frogs, I assume—are sacrificed in secondary-school science classrooms and that in California, Maine, and Pennsylvania students may legally eschew dissection without affecting their grades. The chapter then lists medical schools that do not use lab animals and gives an address for obtaining a list of veterinary schools that offer alternatives to dissections.

When I was ten, I dissected my first leopard frog, a wrinkly specimen pickled in formalin, part of a "Little Mister Biology" kit that my parents gave me for Hanukkah, a kit that also included a crayfish and an earthworm and the mundane but useful tools of the trade—pins, scalpel, tweezers, scissors, microscope, glass slides, and cover slips. A wonderful gift, the biology kit satisfied my inchoate curiosity about what lay beneath a frog's taut and shapely skin. Isn't there more of a frog inside than outside? I prospected for organs. Scalpel and tweezers became my pick and shovel, and I opened the frog's body cavity to seek its buried treasure—kidneys, pancreas, lungs—as intently as if I had been searching for the Lost Dutchman's Mine. That crude mining job led me, eventually, to a course in comparative anatomy, a tour through the atlas of vertebrate evolution, which I completed during my junior year in college after having successfully dissected and memorized the insides of a dogfish, a perch, a bullfrog, a turtle, a lizard, a pigeon, and a cat.

In 1962, several years after I had opened my first leopard frog, I dissected a big, green, slippery bullfrog that I'd caught in a pond and then pithed with a long-handled pin. It was a dreamy, timeless August afternoon at parochial camp in Torrington, Connecticut, where we attended Sabbath service, played baseball, and pithed frogs. The Yankees were in first place, as I remember.

The operation traumatized both the bullfrog and me. As if executing the closing move of a bullfight, I pushed the pin into the frog's head, between and behind its bulbous eyes, which blinked and bobbed at the surface of its skull like corks on a fishing line. I wanted to cut the spinal cord, to disconnect all motor activity so as to have a comatose frog, dead but breathing. But, no matador, I missed the mark. Instead of lying in the dissecting pan, with its heart still pumping but its body limp as jello, the bullfrog squirmed free, leaped to the floor, and hopped across the room, a tiny, nightmarish lance waving from its skull.

I went after it. After catching the frog, I held it tightly in one hand and rotated the pin back and forth, working it like a stick shift. Little bones broke. Eventually, the frog relaxed.

Opening the bullfrog, I found a pink heart that still pulsed, a dark purple liver, yellow globs of fat, several thousand eggs crammed in two long oviducts on either side of the body, and soft, bubble-textured lungs. The white inner skin was lined red with capillaries, like a road map. Prying the frog's mouth open, I scraped my finger along its blunt, vomerine teeth and touched its sticky wad of a tongue. Then, like Marquette and Joliet searching for the Mississippi delta, I traveled downstream through a stomach brimful with baby painted turtles, along the short, coiled intestines where bits of undigested insect shells were coalescing into scat, and eventually out the cloaca into daylight.

Although I oppose animal testing by cosmetic companies, frog dissection, like reading *Moby Dick* or *The Canterbury Tales*, is more than an academic rite of passage. It is a trip back more than 300 million years to the steamy Upper Carboniferous period, the origin of both amphibians and lungs, when our distant ancestors crept out of tepid swamps onto dry land; it is a look at soft tissue—tissue organized and arranged by function, like a self-sustaining ecosystem—a glimpse of complex, fragile nature. It saddens me to think dissection might be excised from school curricula, replaced with sterile, sanitary videos that will interrupt the flow of life and wonder far more than a pith pin. Life science without dissection, the primordial field trip, is science without life.

Busy, lacking patience, we substitute tightly edited half-hour documentaries and video dissections for communion with nature. Although we love watching predation and killing on television, we rail against other people's urge to hunt, whether for sport or to control an overpopulated, starved herd of deer. We say we cannot accept the extinction of an ancient species. Meanwhile, we tolerate the desiccation and development of our remaining wetlands from the central valley of California to the prairie potholes of

North Dakota to the Florida Everglades—wetlands that, if protected, would provide sanctuary to far more than six million
frogs.

Watching and handling living things as they are transformed
from living to dead serves us intellectually, maybe even spiritually,
in ways that are just as basic as the ways a hare serves the bobcat
and a grouse serves the goshawk. Open a leopard frog and with
very little imagination you can see yourself alive and evolved:
your heart, your lungs, your intestines, your cream-white ovaries
preparing for another generation.

Trade Routes
from Another Century

Mark Humpal, a traditional leather craftsman and one of New Hampshire's few buyers of wild fur, works a skinning knife the way someone else might work a pencil: easy, fluid motions, never self-conscious, always meticulous. He guides me down the inside of a sidewinder.

Stretching the skin between thumb and forefinger, I coax the knife around each ventral scale, carefully scraping away moist bits of rattlesnake meat. Mark encourages me. Several weeks before, I had peeled this thin, fragile skin off a Mojave road kill, a two-button male, methodically working my fingernails between flesh and hide, the way you peel an orange. When I had pressed my thumb against the sidewinder's cloaca to free the anal scales, his hemipenis, forked and spiked, popped up like Sir Galahad's mace. I keep the skin, and others like it, to remind me of North America's biologic and geographic contrasts, of land seemingly worlds away from Vermont—hot, dry country, whose geology is emphatic.

I wipe pale pieces of sidewinder meat against the edge of a weathered barn board, then resume the slow process of fleshing, a cross between meditating and shaving, until I scrape the last overlapping ventral scale. Finished, I show the snake to Mark, who caresses the skin with his knife, effortlessly freeing more meat. I had brought Mark three sidewinders and a South Dakota prairie rattlesnake, all scavenged in good shape from western highways, then skinned, salted, rolled scroll-like, and stored in Ziploc plastic bags. Some of these skins I've kept for as long as three years. To prepare the rattlesnakes for tanning, Mark soaked the hides overnight in a bucket of fresh water.

Mark Humpal lives at the end of a dirt road, not far from the Connecticut River. A "Deer Skins" sign announces the turn. On one side of the road lies his hide barn, decorated with tattered bear skins and a weathered moose skull with broad, palmate antlers. In front of the barn, a corrugated steel roof arranged with skulls, jaws, and leg bones from horses, cows, bears, beaver, moose, deer, coyotes, and foxes is anchored against the wind by two old, half-round floor joists and various and sundry rocks pried from the garden. Across the road, rising from a ragged meadow, is his shop-in-progress, a two-story A-frame built with heavy timbers and held together by homemade locust pins. Three ancient posts that once supported a local church's choir loft hold the rafter system and are full of songs, Mark claims; a twenty-foot black cherry collar tie, with a huge burl that from a distance looks like the belly-bulge of a satisfied snake, traverses the roof from side to side.

Behind the shop, Mark's daughters play in a sandpile with brightly colored plastic trucks and beaver-chewed sticks from a nearby dam. On a crossbeam of a tool shed, four robin eggs nestle in a nest of mud, leaves, shop insulation, and cast-off deer hair.

Mark donates materials to birds who, like himself, build with what's available.

Besides my snakes, other skins soak in buckets or lie stretched and tacked on fleshing boards at the head of the driveway: two eastern diamondbacks, one over five feet long; a western diamondback; a bushmaster; an eight-foot boa; a milk snake, which had been injudiciously bludgeoned for "the children's sake" by a neighbor (whose dog had bitten Mark's youngest daughter twice); a Mexican iguana; and a snapping turtle. A pink plastic turtle lies between the bushmaster and the western diamondback.

I nail a brass tack through the skin outside one sidewinder's eye-hole, stretch the skin against the tack, then nail another opposite the first. I repeat the process until the snake is pinned to the board, flesh side up, with fifteen pairs of tacks. Mark inspects. Set the tacks at a more oblique angle, he tells me, leaning away like tent pegs, then, as the skin dries and tightens, it won't pull them out. I oblige. After resetting the tacks, I paint the skin with a mixture of rubbing alcohol and glycerin, place it in the sun to dry, and start fleshing another sidewinder, a six-button female.

Mark Humpal is forty-one, tall, sinewy, with ringlets of brown hair which touch his shoulders, a moustache, sparse beard, and brown sparkling eyes. Today, his blue T-shirt reads "Mixed Breed Regatta." Boats aside, the inscription is revealing. Like a son of the Pleistocene, Mark brain-tans hides, eats salvaged tongues and neck meat, makes deer- and moose-hoof rattles, and trades along ancient routes. Around the Great Lakes, he brings otter pelts to Ojibwa, Swampy Cree, and Potawatomi, and returns with quill-embroidered birch bark and vessels woven of sweet grass. When spring begins to thaw the Northeast, Mark becomes his western alter ego and heads to Arizona, where his leather trader's trail began more than twenty years ago, to barter fox tails and deer hooves to the Hopi for pots, baskets, and Katchina dolls, and to the Yaqui for moth cocoon leg rattles: a series of big, silk cocoons, each one holding a few anthill-pebbles, stitched in sequence to a rawhide stape. One spring he returned to the desert to set his brother's ashes adrift across Papago land.

Mark spent a fatherless boyhood in Waterloo, Iowa, often in the company of his maternal grandparents, Joe and Stella Kopache, who had fled Bohemia. He called them Apache and thought he was Indian until he was ten. Now, he is more indigenous in his ways than many Indians. He believes in indomitable spirits, even in rocks. When his wife of ten years left him, he mailed her the first apple to appear on a tree they had planted years before. He thanks the animals whose flesh he trims, whose hides he tans, whose bodies he incorporates into his art.

"We're all working from a short deck, subject to change without notice," he assures me, while slicing a dollop of rattlesnake meat from the smaller of the two eastern diamondbacks. "I learn as I go."

Mark loves otters; their soft, dense fur has more than thirty thousand hairs per square inch. Vermont's Abenaki love them, too, and wrap their braids with pieces of Humpal-tanned otter. "I try to live my life with integrity. If the otter population was in trouble, I'd stop buying skins."

Outside the garage, two crows escort a turkey vulture beyond the greening hills.

I flesh, stretch, tack, and tan the second and third sidewinders, then begin the prairie rattler, a three-foot long, eight-button male—an ideal hatband—that has a lot more meat stuck to it than the smaller rattlers. It's slow going and tedious. "You've got the knack," Mark tells me, sounding as much like a Little League coach as a craftsman.

An hour later, when I finally finish the last snake, I get up from the table and inventory the garage. I'm surrounded by animals, asunder: two bristly boar hides and a moose neck rolled and stored on a rafter; seven inside-out eastern coyotes; eight gray foxes and seventeen red foxes hanging in a corner from three steel rings, waiting to be shipped to a San Francisco tannery; the mounted head of a pronghorn, white with time and dust-covered; three whitetail heads, with inquisitive glass eyes; and a black duck, wings arched back, legs extended, eternally preparing to land. There are crates of assorted bones and antlers; bottles of bear oil and deer and lamb tallow; tubes of deer hides, rolled flesh-side out; and a bucket of moose legs, each hoof thrust toward heaven.

A side door leads from the garage to Mark's temporary store where glass museum cases are filled with Indian crafts. I wander in. An Iroquois snapping turtle rattle stops me. Grasping the handle, which is the animal's stiff, extended, leather-bound neck, I shake a turtle the color of mud, whose dried, grinning head appears almost alive. Choke cherry pits tumble in the hollow shell, rasping like winter oak leaves.

On the road to Odanak, the Abenaki reservation northeast of Montreal, Mark tells me a story.

On a March night in western New Mexico, a barn owl collided with a car and crashed, beak to the pavement. Cold and still as a stone, the body waited for Mark, an inveterate road-kill collector, to lift it from the highway and use it in a way befitting to a dead owl, in a way that honored it as a symbol of renewal. Owl in the back seat, he drove west to the Hopi reservation, crossing into Arizona beneath a black and starry sky. The bird was to be a gift for two elders, peach farmers, who would fasten its feathers to flowering branches to set the blossoms, invite the bees, and protect the fruit, a Hopi ritual as basic as watering a garden.

Although science might scoff at this relationship between a barn owl and a peach tree, a bond exists, according to the Hopi; the relevant triumvirate also includes the farmer, who is an essential, ineluctable participant. For the Hopi, barn owls are sacred. For me, owls are beautiful, exquisitely adapted for the black hours of night, birds whose eyes and ears work in concert to apprehend the nocturnal landscape. But I am too scientific, too pragmatic, too precise, too busy to place their feathers in my fruit trees. Why should I? My apple trees and blueberry bushes bear fruit. For all my ecological bent, I am still environmentally estranged, an observer of nature who often has an intermediary, either a camera or a pair of binoculars, between himself and the rest of the world. I tell myself I want intimacy with nature, to engage the brook, the meadow, and the long, low line of hills, to see the contours of the land with the clarity of a circling hawk. I want to know where the weasel sleeps, where the oriole weaves her nest. I want to feel at home in the valley, to be sustained and tutored by the seasons, my whole being tuned to subtle shifts of day length, like a raven or a rose-breasted grosbeak, whose survival depends on accuracy. And yet I must continue to load film to help pay our bills.

Driving on toward Odanak, Mark sees a dancer's rattle on the shoulder of the road. I see a dead turtle. Unfortunately for Mark, this one is beyond repair; it's a wood turtle with a handsomely incised shell and orange feet, but she's cracked down the center of the carapace, plastron fractured, scrambled eggs spilling out.

Stopping in Swanton, Vermont, close to the Canadian border, we visit a band of Western Abenaki, "the People of the Dawn," whose ancestors named the region's rivers and hills. Now this is a community adrift, a tribe without legal standing, essentially ignored by both state and federal government and suffering a collective midlife crisis. Most of the people busying themselves inside the Abenaki Activity Center are women. A blond teenager sits by a phone that doesn't ring. Dorcas, our chaperone, her short red hair and cool blue eyes as Irish as a leprechaun's, shows us a dis-

play case that holds several small dyed and embroidered ash baskets, an ax, a birch-bark fan, soapstone pipes, and two African
skin drums, which Mark recognizes as misplaced.

Later, Susan, a cherubic social worker in her late forties, with
permed blond tresses touching her shoulders, who thinks her maternal grandmother "might" have had some Indian blood, takes us
to see two crude totem poles that lie across sawhorses in a shed
behind the community center next to a grain elevator. The smell
of fermented corn is everywhere and powerful. A gift from the
Abenaki to the town, one of the totems eventually will be planted
on the Swanton green, as geographically and ethnically out of
place as serving bagels and lox at a San Genaro festival, which underscores how bruised and diluted this culture really is.

Susan inquires whether Cuprinol is the best preservative for
sealing the wood. Mark suggests bear oil and reminds her that
totem poles are not made to last forever.

"Bear oil?"

Brushing my fingers over a carved wooden wolf with fore-
shortened legs which looks more like a gray squirrel than a wild
canid, I ask Susan what brought her to Vermont.

"Oh, the back-to-Earth sort of thing."

We leave Swanton, cross into Quebec, and lunch at a strawberry farm. A dozen barn swallows seine gnats above a pasture
orange with hawkweed.

Crossing the St. Francis River, we enter Odanak. The men
with whom Mark trades are not home so we go to the Abenaki
Culture Museum, which turns out to be a euphemism for the Je-
suit-Missionaries-Saved-Their-Souls Museum. At the end of a series of dioramas that feature some of North America's worst
taxidermy is the recreation of a missionary classroom: an immaculate room with four oiled desks, and a display case, the finest in
the entire museum, that holds a single rosary. A mannequin
dressed as a nun at the head of the classroom leans into an open

book that reads "Jesus" and "Repent" in bold black letters. Vacant-faced Abenaki kids, a lost generation, stare from a 1910 class picture that hangs behind the nun.

Later in the afternoon, we find Fred the Carver sipping beer in a Pierreville tavern. He's all Abenaki, a powerful man, broad shouldered and potbellied, with a boxer's nose and short, thick fingers. He wears a turquoise tank top. He invites us home. Fred moved to Odanak from Albany, and after years of working construction took a course in carving and native crafts and began moonlighting as a craftsman. He left his family behind. For company, he has two squabbling parakeets, one blue, the other green. Vinyl flooring curls in the kitchen. Mark admires a brown ash vessel, for which he offers two ermine pelts and a small ironwood turtle, a Hopi icon. Fred handles the ermine, like a kid running sand through his fingers, then consummates the deal.

Next, Mark unrolls two big brain-tanned New Hampshire beavers that Fred praises but for which he has no use.

"I traded for a deer skin two years ago that still just sits by the TV. What would I do with them?"

On the kitchen counter a curved ash cane with a stuffed-bald-eagle-head handle waits for its owner, an Abenaki from Swanton. Its white feathers gray with age, this eagle head was twisted off a mounted bird stolen from the lobby of a Vermont hotel.

Last April, after a failed eighteen-month United States Fish and Wildlife Service sting operation in which undercover agents tried to tempt Mark Humpal to sell or buy illegal wildlife—out-of-state and out-of-season animals, untagged fur bearers, or animals with restricted commercial use—a judge issued a warrant at the behest of a federal warden to search Mark's house and shop. The federal agents confiscated the skins of two road-killed gila monsters, three katchina dolls with unidentified down feathers, two golden eagle claws—purchased twenty years ago from an ad in a

Southwest Indian magazine—and a page from Mark's journal that recounts the story of the road-killed owl and the peach farmers. Transporting a protected species, dead or alive, across state lines is a federal infraction. These personal items, totems, like a crucifix or a Star of David, remind Mark of the unnameable force that forged the Earth. If an Indian can become a Jew or a Catholic, why does a white man, who interacts deeply and devoutly with nature, get persecuted for his beliefs?

Mark helps Swanton's Abenaki discover their past, trades with them, teaches them. He helps them to mend their splintered culture. With limited funds in the federal coffer, why was so much time, effort, and money spent to apprehend a man who still draws an honest living from nature, a kind of farmer? Writing about the glory of fly fishing, W. D. Wetherell laments that today's technocrat "is sick to death because of the artificial divisions he has established between himself and the natural world. Anything that gets us past these divisions is worthy of passionate pursuit, whether it be the flowers of a suburban gardener or the birds of the amateur ornithologist."

Trading with natives, Mark follows grooves in prehistoric paths. A smiling black bear skull sits on an oil drum, waiting for a trip west to the Hopi, waiting for Mark's return.

The Electrical
Watershed

The sound of our photoelectric thermal curtains rising with the daylight had awakened me, but as fog moved up the valley, the curtains closed. Each change in the density of the fog triggered the curtains' sensitive eye. They closed. They opened. Closed, again. Annoyed with the prospect of being able neither to return to sleep nor to watch the landscape uninterrupted, I turned off the photoelectric cell, leaving the curtains permanently open.

When the fog bank started to slowly retreat, the valley emerged like a Polaroid picture. Distant lines that suggested hills, became hills. I saw a great blue heron standing near the pond, its gaze fixed on the water. The scene evoked wildness, an eminent bird poised by a seemingly obscure pond.

But the view was misleading, ambiguous, for we live on the antiseptic end of a titanic electrical conduit. I had our electric lines buried, hiding our link to the Bradford substation, to give the valley a sense of remoteness. What is the real price we'll pay for our energy-innovative, high-tech curtains?

From my seat on the jet, I saw northern Quebec stretch below. Rivers flowed across granite and muskeg, while wind-furrowed water shimmied in the middle of open bogs. Stunted evergreens crept up barren, glacier-polished hills and sandy eskers. We passed over cold lakes of innumerable shapes and sizes, light brown in the shallows, darker with depth; one looked like a goose about to land, wings up and neck extended, another like a dodo standing on its head. An access road and the world's largest power line right-of-way, as wide as U.S. Interstate 80, severed the scene.

I was aboard an Air Creebec charter with thirteen other environmentalists: eleven from Vermont, two from Massachusetts. We were guests of Hydro-Quebec—Quebec's government-owned electric company, which is one of the two largest nonfinancial corporations in Canada—and the Grand Council of the Cree. Eleven Hydro-Quebec biologists, engineers, and publicists escorted us in flight, interpreting the scenery and answering our questions about the price of electrical power.

We spent three days in Radisson, the heart of Hydro-Quebec's La Grande River Complex, and three days with the Cree along the shores of James Bay and Hudson Bay. Both groups wanted to win us over as allies. The Cree hope to stop further hydro-construction, while Hydro-Quebec hopes to sell Vermont more "cheap, clean, renewable energy." Utility officials assumed that our minds were open to a case for "taming the north," that we might be convinced to embrace some sort of manifest cultural and ecological destiny in the name of lower electric rates.

Yet, this was the most biased group I've ever traveled with. Expecting us to buy into such a radical, Earth-altering scheme, one that would transfigure a swath of northern Quebec as large as western Europe and as fragile as spun glass, so that we could race into an incandescent future surrounded by time-saving electrical gadgets, was preposterous.

With 53 generating stations, 16,800 miles of transmission lines, and 56,400 miles of medium voltage lines, Hydro-Quebec generates, transmits, and distributes more than 90 percent of the province's electricity, satisfying the electric appetite of more than three million households and businesses. Seventy-one percent of Quebec residences—more than 90 percent of all new homes—are heated by electricity.

According to Prime Minister Robert Bourassa, "Quebec is a vast hydro-electric plant in the bud, and every day, millions of potential kilowatt hours flow downhill and out to the sea. What a waste!" To harness this energy, Hydro-Quebec has established a twenty-year game plan that includes diverting or damming twenty large rivers and more than four hundred small rivers to produce a series of reservoirs that will drown five thousand square miles of land and have a combined total surface area larger than Lake Ontario. In the end, Hydro-Quebec will have altered the drainage pattern of nearly three hundred thousand square miles of boreal woods and muskeg, eviscerating a wilderness four and a half times larger than New England.

Actually, Bourassa sees more to the north than potential megawatts. He sees power. In his book, *Power from the North,* Bourassa endorses the GRAND (Great Recycling and Northern Development) Canal, a scheme to build a hundred-mile-long dike across the mouth of James Bay, closing it off from Hudson Bay and creating a vast freshwater reservoir. He envisions diverting— he calls it recycling—the three million gallons per second that flow into James Bay to the Great Lakes, then exporting water to the thirsty western heartland. The scope of both Hydro-Quebec's electrical conquest and the GRAND Canal makes the Tennessee Valley Authority appear like sandbox engineering.

More than nine hundred miles of crackling transmission lines tie New England to Radisson. By the year 2000, Hydro-Quebec expects to export 10 percent of its electrical output, primarily to New York and New England. Vermont taps into this network, bleeding electricity from the Comerford substation. In mid-October 1990, Vermont agreed to buy more power. An electrical transfusion of 450 megawatts would supply about 3 billion kilowatt hours, enough juice to run 375,000 homes for a year.

Hydro-Quebec has already begun gutting eastern North America's last and largest wilderness. Of the nine rivers that were diverted to increase the flow of the La Grande, the Opinaca and the Eastmain have been reduced to a dribble at their mouths. The LG 2 powerhouse in Radisson produces 10,000 megawatts a year, which is about half of the power generated in New England from all sources combined—hydro, oil, coal, nuclear, solar, and wind—and about seven times as that generated by the Hoover Dam, the largest hydroelectric dam in the United States.

As I watched waves lap the shore of LG 2, a reservoir three times larger than Lake Champlain, it occurred to me that in fifteen years the government-owned utility company may have had a more drastic impact on northern Quebec than the melting of the last glacier.

Beginning in 1978, as a part-time faculty member in the Environmental Science Department at New England College, I taught a freshman course called "Man and the Environment." Considered a general science elective by the curriculum committee, "Man" was almost always filled, for students found it far less threatening than either physics or chemistry.

A depressing class to teach, "Man and the Environment" focused on a panoply of environmental ills, each one compressed and served as a week-long unit: human population dynamics, world hunger and food resources, urbanization, nonrenewable metal and mineral resources: are we running out?, the energy crisis, the greenhouse effect, noise pollution, water pollution, air pollution, endangered species, and so on. From week to week, there was little relief from the litany of crises I asked the class to consider.

One bright spot in the course was Boyce Richardson's film, *Cree Hunters of Mistassini*, a documentary of life in a communal winter hunting camp on the La Grande River watershed, seven hundred miles north of Montreal. The Cree offer a startling contrast to the way Western culture views both land and time. For the copper-faced Cree, land is not a commodity, and the only relevant time is the present. They do not horde against an uncertain future. The Cree subsist as hunters, indivisible from the rivers and thousands of lakes that lace the gray Canadian Shield and bright green muskeg of northern Quebec. And like caribou and wolves, the Cree move with the seasons.

The documentary follows their route. Three families leave Mistassini, a Cree village on the south end of Lake Mistassini, once so far removed from mainstream Canada that it took seven months for the news of the outbreak of World War I to reach it. They are headed for the winter camp belonging to one of the Crees, Sam Blacksmith. Each of the families has their own territories, but animal populations have become too low to sustain hunting, so they deliberately take a year off their own sparse ground to give the land a reprieve. Sam, whose land has a high population of animals, invites them to hunt and trap with him. We see the Cree build a spruce log cabin chinked with sphagnum, trap beaver, shoot a merganser and a pregnant moose, fish, and tan hides. After hunting they gently hang black bear, lynx, and beaver skulls in a tree to soothe the animal spirits, and smile a lot while living in what might be called abject poverty, sixteen people squashed in one room with plastic windows and no plumbing. Outside, it's forty degrees below zero.

Apparently nobody needs his or her "own space." Kids do not require time-outs. Everybody has a role, everybody helps.

What I did not know in those years that I watched *Cree Hunters of Mistassini* was that the film documented a livelihood in serious jeopardy: the pact between the Cree and their subarctic homeland was already being ruptured by Hydro-Quebec. In 1971, Robert Bourassa had proclaimed that the northern rivers were "wasting away in foam and swirls" and initiated the largest construction project in the history of humanity.

Gaetan Hayeur, director of the environment with Hydro-Quebec, a specialist on anadromous fish and a thick-wristed bear of man, stalked through our days in Radisson like a general watching his troops. Whenever one of our Hydro-Quebec chaperones faltered under a bombardment of questions, Hayeur spoke up. I asked about the George River caribou herd, the largest on the continent.

Before 1940, the caribou herd numbered about two thousand. At that time, the caribou in western Quebec resided only in the campfire stories of the Cree elders. They promised their young audience that one day the animals would return. And in fact, between 1955 and 1982 the George River herd increased at an annual rate of 14 percent per year and returned to the lowlands west of Hudson Bay.

Now, each year, a massive herd of more than seven hundred thousand caribou, tawny-colored Ice Age deer, migrate across northern Quebec. After calving in the fog and stunted spruce along the Labrador border, the herd fractures into smaller and smaller bands which move west along the interior rivers that serve as frozen highways through barren ground. Caribou depend on shorelines for their food, feeding in the woods growing close to shore on gray-green reindeer lichen, their principal food. According to Hayeur, the herd had grown so large that they exhausted the lichen on the calving grounds; the only place it grows is between boulders where the animals cannot reach it. The herd must therefore migrate soon after calving.

Hayeur claimed that the Hydro-Quebec reservoirs helped to return caribou to western Quebec by expanding shorelines with the five hundred mile chain of artificial lakes on the La Grande River, opening virgin lichen mats to the animals. Some caribou calve on the new islands, he said, taking pressure off the traditional calving ground.

In early September 1984, Hydro-Quebec finished filling Caniapiscau Reservoir, a man-made lake the size of Delaware. Three weeks later and three hundred miles below the dam, ten thousand twisted caribou rode the seething river over Calcaire Falls and littered the shoreline up to forty-five miles downstream, victims of heavy September rains that had overflowed the spillway at Duplanter and swept them away as they crossed the river at their usual spot. Could the spillway have been closed and the water diverted? There was no need, said Hayeur, for the flow at Calcaire Falls in late September 1984 was less than it would have been without the reservoir. He showed me figures prepared by Hydro-Quebec biologists that corroborate his position, figures that are disputed by Cree and Inuit and nongovernment biologists. In a statement more suited to a *National Enquirer* headline than to a provincial government report, Hydro-Quebec proclaimed that "God killed the caribou."

The Cree disagreed. They claimed that lichen, caribou, and wolf populations vary naturally over the centuries and that the high point of the caribou population happens to have coincided with the biggest construction project in the history of humankind. After five thousand years of hunting and gathering in the Quebec wilderness, the Cree's opinion should be reliable—their roots run deeper than the shallow northern soil would seem to permit.

Sixty miles west of Radisson, the La Grande River empties into James Bay. Close by, the Cree village of Chisasibi limps into the twenty-first century. Hydro-Quebec and the federal government spent $50 million to build Chisasibi when the La Grande, delivering twice its former volume of water after geographic surgery, began to subsume nearby Fort George Island, the local Cree's former settlement. More than fifteen hundred people moved from the island to Chisasibi; several dozen refused to leave, preferring instead to be washed into James Bay.

Chisasibi is a prefab community with cluster housing built on subarctic soil so thin that if you sneeze you just about expose bedrock. The community now has almost as many GMC Suburbans as Fairlee, Vermont. I saw a boy riding a yellow mountain bike, girls in black high tops, boys in white, a cemetery littered with red plastic flowers, a Roman Catholic church, a hockey rink with a twisted steel frame, two satellite dishes, a fax machine, a canoe shop, a small hospital, and an unfinished community center shaped like a tepee. A gray cinder-block high school erupts with students at 3:00 P.M. In an olive-green, aluminum-sided mall, Cree elders played checkers and shoppers bought neon sneaker laces, New Kids on the Block posters, pineapple upside-down cake, and greeting cards that said, "Happy Birthday to the Chief, With You Around It's No Wonder the Rest of Us Are Just Indians." In the parking lot outside the mall, two women wearing greasy coats hawked Nevada Royale lottery tickets from a shopping cart near a sign that read: "$75 Fine for Littering." Losing tickets drifted by.

Outside Chisasibi, a taut sphagnum mat stretched across an old lake. A plateau of dwarf, wind-twisted black spruce yielded to a carpet of arctic wildflowers, which in turn yielded to the yawning mud flats of James Bay. Jack pine crowded sandy eskers. A black-spotted American toad with one bulging Peter Lorre–like eye crouched in arctic duff, and beyond, a flock of whistling greater yellowlegs dipped toward the bay. Bright green tendrils of willow and alder traced the banks of a small river. Everywhere, the three-billion-year-old Canadian Shield, as old and cold as the moon, butted up through the veneer of vegetation.

For the Cree, one of the most recently affected indigenous people in the world, the hunting and gathering life has worked continuously for millennia. In 1972, only 20 percent of the Cree were wage earners, and the rest lived off the land, working their trap lines, hunting, and fishing either full or part-time. During the first two weeks of August, nearly every Fort George resident gathered to net spawning whitefish on the first rapids of the La Grande River, the future site of LG 2. During that winter, inland Cree harvested 891 moose, which accounted for 50 percent of their winter diet.

Many Cree are still subsistence hunters, living on a land that, until very recently, no one else wanted. In spring and fall, they hunt the migrating waterfowl, snow and Canada geese, brant, and ducks of every stripe, that feed by the millions in the James Bay lowlands. In the summer, they fish for squaretails, lake trout, cisco, Arctic char, whitefish, northern pike, walleye, and lake sturgeon. In the winter, they trap beaver, muskrat, lynx, red fox, marten, mink, ermine, and otter. The Cree eat duck eggs in June; guillemot chicks in August; willow ptarmigan in December and March; and snowshoe hare, spruce grouse, and snowy owl, which they call "northern chicken" and which is as chewy and pungent as Michael Jordan's sneakers, in October. The black bear and moose hunt begins in late August, the caribou hunt in October, and the porcupine hunt when crowberry ripens in September. Coastal Cree hunt beluga whales in June and July, seals until November ice-up, and polar bears on that rare occasion when one wanders into the neighborhood.

Said Robbie Dick, Chief of the Great Whale Cree: "A lot of

our people still depend on a way of life off the land. Even those of us who have full employment in the communities, we still go out and practice that tradition when time permits. We don't go down to sunny Florida and lay in the sun on our holidays. We go out there and practice our tradition, most of the people do. This is something we want to hold on to."

Since the end of the Ice Age, mercury locked in the Canadian Shield has slowly weathered out and washed into northern lakes, collecting in substantial quantities in the sediment. There, it bonds with methane produced by respiring anaerobic bacteria and enters the aquatic food chain as methyl mercury, an extremely toxic compound that, on entering the human body, attacks kidneys, liver, and brain, and produces birth defects. The more anaerobic the decomposition, the more methyl mercury.

Having smothered an area the size of Rhode Island under several hundred billion cubic feet of water, LG 2 nurtures an unimaginable quantity of anaerobic bacteria, which busily decompose more than eight hundred thousand acres of drowned spruce and muskeg. From plankton to aquatic insects, from whitefish to pike to humans, mercury courses through the food chain, concentrating at higher levels as it passes from prey to predator, a classic and particularly insidious example of biologic magnification, for methyl mercury is imperceptible to our senses.

Lake whitefish is a long-lived, deep-bottomed, laterally thin fish, iridescent blue to pearly white, with a small mouth and an overhanging snout. Whitefish grow slowly and grow large, more than two feet long and up to forty-two pounds, on a diet of bottom-dwelling aquatic insect larvae and mollusks, as well as midwater floating plankton. During the summer, and at any time when other food species are scarce, many Cree families eat the abundant and delicious whitefish daily. Women traditionally wean their babies with a juice made of pulverized whitefish which is sucked through a hollow, goose-quill straw from a gourd made of a pike's stomach.

After the completion of the La Grande River Complex, reservoir-dwelling and downstream whitefish became dangerously tainted with mercury. In 1983, three years after the LG 2 reservoir had been filled, the amount of mercury in whitefish flesh had risen 225 percent, from 0.16 milligrams per kilogram to 0.52 milligrams per kilogram. In 1989, the fish still carried three times more mercury than they did before the building of the reservoir. Northern pike, a long-lived predator with razor teeth and a voracious appetite, had accumulated six times more mercury than whitefish.

In 1988, after several Cree hair samples yielded 18 milligrams per kilogram of mercury, the Cree Board of Health declared all predatory fish caught in LG 2, including burbot, lake trout, walleye, northern pike, and all species caught below the reservoir unfit for human consumption. They also recommended that women of child-bearing age stop eating predatory fish taken out of the La Grande River, the longest, widest, most important river in Cree country.

Nicole Chartrand, head of Hydro-Quebec's Department of Environment and Public Health told me that the mercury guidelines for fish consumption in the James Bay area set by the James Bay Mercury Committee were not as strict as those set by the World Health Organization. "If Indians listened to the World Health Organization, no one would eat fish."

From my days teaching "Man and the Environment," I recall these sobering facts: Between 1953 and 1960, Minamata, Japan, introduced the world to the effects of accumulated methyl mercury when 52 people died and 150 suffered debilitating brain damage after eating contaminated fish. In 1972, when Iraqi villagers baked bread with grain coated with a fungicide made of methyl mercury, 459 died and more than 6500 were seriously injured. Will the Cree be the next case study in the effects of mercury poisoning, or have thousands of years of incremental exposure to methyl mercury translated into a higher tolerance?

At Hydro-Quebec's mercury monitoring laboratory in Radisson, I watched biologists autopsy LG 2 fish and then discuss fish consumption. The mercury level in fish from the Canadian Shield is naturally high, they said, and in ten to fifteen years the level in reservoir fish will return to normal. They failed to report, however, that the deep, organic peatlands that dominate the La Grande drainage store great quantities of mercury and release this accumulation over a much longer period of time than does a flooded spruce forest.

To date, Hydro-Quebec biologists have autopsied more than twenty thousand fish, and their findings are not good. Cree are advised not to eat more than two meals of whitefish per week for five to ten years after construction of LG 2; then five meals per week twenty years after, and nine meals each week at thirty years. The prognosis for pike is, lined with mercury, these fish make better thermometers than food. The biologists have warned against eating more than two meals of pike per week for thirty years after completion of LG 2.

Yet, unwilling to relinquish a five thousand-year-old tradition, many Cree still set nets in the rapids below the dam.

Those fileted whitefish, skin peeled back to reveal a distended bag of eggs, were nothing like the tasty Sunday morning whitefish, smoked to a greasy golden-brown, that my father brought home from Rosenbaum's Kosher Deli. These are riddled with methyl mercury. No one takes whitefish home from the lab for dinner.

Four months later, at a seminar on the effects of methyl mercury seminar at Dartmouth College, a toxicologist who had thoroughly analyzed, externalized, and objectified the situation, reminded those in attendance of the Alar scare several years ago, of how easy it was for the middle class to give up apples when faced with the threat of cancer. He insisted on the ease with which the Cree can turn away from fish and employ other options for protein. Spam, perhaps.

Able to replace apples with an almost infinite array of grocery fruits, going without does not make me suffer. Apples have never winged me to nirvana. Although I pick apples in October, I do not engage in blooming or pruning or grafting ceremonies at the local orchard on Wild Hill, nor do I dance about the stove while Linny bakes apple brown Betty. But perhaps I should, for only when I am devoted to apples—or any other locally grown food, for that matter—will I comprehend the Crees' sacrifice. Or really taste my own valley.

What if the entire Connecticut River was spaded, diverted, dammed to provide energy for North Carolina, which is as far away from my home ground as I am from the La Grande River? What if Blood Brook hemorrhaged behind a dam and our valley was swallowed by a wall of water, and I could no longer live as a self-employed naturalist because of the skewed idea that progress and convenience are synonymous? Then I would feel the dilemma of the Cree.

From the open door of a Hydro-Quebec helicopter, I looked across LG 2, across coves choked by flotillas of spruce which pile and rot in the shallows. I saw the 2700-foot-long spillway carved in the Canadian Shield, a granite staircase with 13 steps, each one 400 feet wide and 33 feet tall. When the gates open to release spring runoff, the spillway surges with the combined flow of all the rivers in Europe, twice the volume of water of the St. Lawrence River at Montreal, water rich with methyl mercury.

Behind the spillway, a 500-foot-high stone dam, larger than fifty-four thousand two-story houses, garrotes the La Grande

River. One Cree elder told me that increased precipitation has followed the building of the reservoirs—a claim Hydro-Quebec disputes—and that one day the dam at LG 2 will break and Chisasibi will disappear like Pompei.

In an effort to provide cheap electricity to the Northeast, the cathedral of the Cree has been flooded. Once an avenue, the La Grande River is now an obstacle. Since the amount of water the river discharges into James Bay fluctuates with demand for electricity in the south, the river is no longer cyclical and comprehensible. The La Grande now surges in the winter to provide peak power, then slows in spring as reservoirs recharge with snow melt and rain. Now, ice-out begins in January instead of May. Daily fluctuations occur, too. Cree routinely fall through slush holes in the ice when winter water levels change overnight. The sturgeon have left the La Grande. And the alder-willow flood plain, the best wildlife habitat along any northern river, has washed away or is underwater. Beaver are scarce. Ptarmigan are scarce. And Cree ancestors rest in crypts under icy water.

Why do strangers devour their land? Why do the powerless pay for our electrical conveniences? In 1972, Christopher D. Stone, a law professor from the University of Southern California, wrote an essay for the *Southern California Law Review* that proposed giving legal rights to "natural objects," a novel idea at the time. Today we broker entire watersheds and biologic provinces, and lament the passing of climate and the ozone layer. Just beyond our doorstep, the northern tier of the continent drowns as we luxuriate in incandescent madness.

LG 2, the world's largest underground generating station, descends more than four hundred feet into the Canadian Shield and opens into an immaculate room, a quarter of a mile long, with an arched, rough-hewn ceiling of ancient granite. Sixteen large orange cabinets, each filled with state-of-the-art electrical equipment, each located above one of the sixteen turbines that converts the power of flowing water into electricity, lined the windowless, tubular room with bright relief and me with despair.

On a cool catwalk that dripped condensation, I peered down into a grim and foamy oracle. Angry water racing below me, roaring through a solid granite penstock at nearly a million gallons a second, drove the turbines that converted and discharged electricity to the Radisson substation, that transmitted highways of energy to Montreal, to Vermont. To me.

I stood inside the LG 2 control room. Behind me, a bulletproof window looked across to a twenty-first-century facade. Facing me was a wall full of switches and panels and flashing lights. Deep in a hole in the ground, with all the controls in one little room, I felt like Jack Lemmon in the movie *The China Syndrome*. Too bad I could not commandeer LG 2 with Nikon F3s and Fujichrome film and reverse this subarctic insanity. But the momentary transgression of fantasy was delicious.

Four days later, traveling in a Cree canoe along the coast of Hudson Bay, forty miles north of the village of Whapmagoostui on the mouth of the Grande Baleine River, I visited the site of the proposed spillway for Hydro-Quebec's phase two, the Great Whale Project. This was virgin land, untamed frontier. An immature bald eagle passed, and a flock of black ducks, then a scattering of black guillemots, white wings gleaming. I stopped at a goose hunting camp where mats of cranberry, crowberry and reindeer lichen stretched from a patchy, rock-studded spruce woods. Two immature merlins sliced through the spruce as a songbird's heart speeded up. A red helicopter blazed with a white circle cut by a shaft of lightning shattered the silence. The surveyors, I was told, working out the logistics for the new spillway.

According to Chief Robbie Dick, Hydro-Quebec researchers, after completing an extensive environmental study, have discussed the supposed effects that river diversion will have on the land, while referring to maps with lake outlets drawn in backwards.

If completed, the Great Whale Project will divert part of the Nastapoka River into the Petite Baleine and part of the Petite Baleine into Grande Baleine through the Coates River; will flood the basins of the Grande Baleine, the Petite Baleine, the Nastapoka, the Coates, and the Boutin rivers; will require construction of three airports, two permanent and one temporary; and will cross ten rivers with an additional 321 miles of roads to produce another 3000 megawatts, mostly for export to the United States. To complete the infrastructure by 1994, Hydro-Quebec needs $500 million, the cost of Vermont's new electric contract. I'm helping to finance this. At the end of 1988, Hydro-Quebec was $21.6 billion in debt. With an interest rate of 10.92 percent, the utility company pays $2.34 billion a year in interest, 45 percent of their total revenue. In 1989, the cost of debt exceeded the return on equity by more than 4 percent. Vermont agreed to help them out.

In 1975, worried they'd lose their land without compensation, the Cree signed the James Bay Agreement, their first treaty ever with Canada, and accepted a settlement of $180 million, the equivalent of $18,000 per person or $1.25 per acre of land. The Inuit settled for $108 million. "All they need to do is take the silver and get out of the way," said a Hydro-Quebec engineer. In return for taking the silver, the Cree relinquished claim to all but 5225 square miles, now called category 1 land, of their 386,000-square-mile wilderness homeland. They have exclusive hunting and fishing rights on an additional 60,000 square miles, called Category 2 land, but Hydro-Quebec retains the mining and water development rights, after further compensation. All the rest of northern Quebec is fair game for the utility company.

The Grand Council of the Cree do not want phase 2 and 3,

or the conversion of James Bay from a productive estuary into a toxic sinkhole. They now deeply regret having signed the James Bay Agreement. As late as August 1990, however, the Inuit still supported the treaty. Of Quebec's 3000 Inuit, only the 150 who live at mouth of the Grande Baleine River will be directly affected by the new construction. The rest were awarded a windfall and were compensated for a loss they did not yet suffer. Of the eighty-two-member Makivik Corporation, the governing board of Quebec Inuit, only six oppose the James Bay Agreement, all of them from Whapmagoostui.

Comparing the scope of the La Grande project to the accomplishments of the New York Philharmonic Symphony, Premier Bourassa said that the river which "today appears to be as natural and uncontroversial as water flowing downhill, is the product of enormous and sustained human effort." Unfortunately, Bourassa's "sustained human effort" has victimized the Cree.

Sitting at a Cree council meeting in Whapmagoostui, an elder waved his hand toward the Hudson Bay fog and commented through an interpreter on his community's supposed revenue from Hydro-Quebec construction jobs.

There will be a lot of work during the construction. And just like fog which comes and then it passes, the same thing will happen. Work will last some time but it will come to an end. When it comes to an end, where we traditionally had hunted will just be underwater, the river and all of the animals will not be there.

Three hundred seventy-two Cree lost their jobs after completion of LG 2, and of Hydro-Quebec's 19,500 present permanent employees, only 150 are Cree.

After a bottle of wine at a gourmet dinner in Radisson, a Hydro-Quebec engineer, who apparently sympathized with my opinions about "other" global environmental issues, told me that this state-of-the-art hydroelectric project will be obsolete and defunct in seventy years, after cheaper sources of electricity are found (and once the dams have silted up too much sludge to pass water).

On November 9, 1965, just after 5:15 P.M., in a chicken-wire cubicle in a corner of the high school basement, surrounded by a coterie of other naked wrestlers who were waiting to check their weight amid the tart smells of fermented sweat clothes, I ceremoniously stepped on the scales. The lights went out. We broke ranks, groped for our lockers, then dressed by braille, sticky with perspiration. Eventually, we worked our way upstairs and discovered that an electrical seizure, rippling from Ontario south through a watershed of transmission lines, had left most of Michigan and the Northeast, from Buffalo to Boston, in darkness. More than thirty million people faced a true night, many for the first time.

I remember that night. Six of us squeezed into Mike Junod's Thunderbird to witness "The Great Blackout of '65." Candles and hurricane lamps flickered from suburban windows. People clenched transistor radios and walked flashlight beams down the sidewalk. Restaurants emptied in midmeal. In my lifetime, the stars above Long Island had never looked so bright.

Now, when I turn my lights on, and when the photoelectric curtains automatically roll up to reveal Blood Brook valley, I remember beautiful, subarctic Quebec and the suffering Cree, their dignity, sincerity, and candor. Perhaps periodic blackouts—like that transitory, enchanted blackness that descended on Long Island twenty-five years ago—might do us all some good.

Epilogue

Tacked to my office wall is a color-coded map, "World Biogeo-graphical Provinces," which describes the distributions of plant and animal communities. Unlike conventional maps with their rigid political boundaries, lines that demarcate biological provinces are mutable and fluid, often with wide transition zones that shift and shimmy with the vagaries of climactic and geologic forces. Grasslands, for instance, province 18, is a bright yellow swath that runs north from the Gulf Coast of Texas into south-central Canada, roughly splitting in half North America, which is called the "nearctic realm" by biogeographers. During wet years, deciduous trees invade the prairie along the eastern border and grasses invade the desert along the southwestern border. During dry years, the process reverses. Sometimes fire nudges a transi-tion zone east or west, depending of course on where it strikes, and driving back the advanced guard of either the desert or the deciduous woods.

I remember a controlled burn of 800 acres of shortgrass on the Llano Estacado, hot, dry country only a bucket of rain away from being part Chihuanhuan desert. On a cool March morning,

200

with the wind blowing lightly toward the Double Mountain fork of the Brazos River, we lit the grass. Flames leaped and raced in twisted orange lines, moving back on themselves with every whoosh of the wind. The desert receded: cholla and prickly pear withered, mesquite burned. A few days later, green tobossa shoots poked through the ash as a small portion of transition zone returned to grass.

Now I live at the northeast corner of province 5, the eastern forest, shown on the map as a pale-green, fist-shaped region crowned by the steel-blue of Canadian taiga, and set upon the deep green of Austroriparian, the humid, alligator-rich bottom lands of the Southeast, province 6. Except for the Hudson and the Mohawk rivers, which appear on the map as unlabeled, wavy lines, there are no discernible features in the northeast corner of province 5. Ten thousand Blood Brooks descend invisibly. Even my watershed's aorta, the Connecticut River, remains nameless and unseen.

Although the nuances of my home ground, the rush and lilt of the brook with its haggard ravens propelled by currents above Bald Top and the trembling gray-green of its young big-toothed aspen leaves, are all subsumed on the map into pale-green uniformity, when I look at the map of "World Biogeographical Provinces" I see a world order that embodies biologic rhythms. This reminds me of my reliance on products that are produced outside of province 5 and, in some cases, outside of the nearctic realm, in regions to which I have little or no visceral connection. I eat oranges grown in province 6, wheat from province 18, raisins and prunes from province 7, smoked salmon from province 1. And so on. My friend Ginger once baked granola from ingredients grown on four continents. My Nikons are assembled in the Japanese evergreen forest from metals mined in the East Siberian taiga and the Brazilian planalto, and from plastics made of Persian Gulf petroleum. The source of chemicals that constitute Fugichrome film remains a mystery to me.

I know neither the conditions of south Florida soil nor the population dynamics of Pacific salmon. Yet, my appetite leaves its marks on the recesses of the globe. Knowing Blood Brook's lore cannot be enough, as the entire world is my grocery. My dietary whims affect even the ozone layer.

I am, according to Raymond Dasmann (author more than thirty years ago of *Biological Conservation*, still in print), a typical "biosphere" person, stockholder in the grand scheme of global economy and technology, loosed from the constraints of my biogeographic province. Earth would be much healthier, wrote Dasmann, if there were more "ecosystem" people who "lived within one ecosystem or, at most, a few closely related ecosystems, and depended entirely on the continued functioning of those ecosystems for their survival." Traditionally, ecosystem people have had intimate, complex relationships between their culture and nature which assure that an individual's economic interests need not jeopardize the health of the surrounding environment. Ecosystem people worship the earth as the basis of life. The subarctic Cree of province 4, for example, are still fairly self-sufficient and nonmaterialistic; the Cree dance for whitefish and sing for moose to join the earth's cycles and patterns, which they caress daily with their myths and ceremonies, researches, and contemplations.

Red knots know the Earth. Synchronized with widely spaced planetary pulses, these plump, red-breasted sandpipers nest along the crown of the globe from Greenland to Scandinavia. Knots migrate down every coastline of the world to winter from Tierra del Fuego to New Zealand. Some populations complete round trips that approach twenty thousand miles. In early May, precisely when the horseshoe crabs spawn, hundreds of thousands of knots arrive at Delaware Bay. For four weeks they fatten on crab eggs. Sated, the red knots conclude their flight to the high arctic. Can I travel like a migratory bird, stopping to feast at different points in the hemisphere, fully engaged in my own evolving patterns? Am I capable of being that finely attuned to more than one biogeographic province?

Our environmental crisis is a crisis of empathy and imagination: we see ourselves as separate from and superior to nature. How else could our addiction to consumption have developed? In *The Great Gatsby*, F. Scott Fitzgerald closed with an evocative image of a moonlit Long Island harbor with a green dock light shining across the water from Daisy's house. The green light signals Earth on a half shell, raw, ready to be consumed. Twenty-five years ago, Lynn White pinpointed the Book of Genesis, chapter 1, verse 28, as the source of the crisis. After blessing Adam and Eve, God announces to the newlyweds: "Be fruitful and multiply, and replenish the earth, and subdue it; and have dominion over the fish of the sea, and over the fowl of the air, and over every living thing that creepeth upon the earth."

Think of Ahab pinioned to the whale, his lifeless arm beckoning the Pequod's crew; a literal approach to the words "subdue" and "dominion" leads us obediently and blindly into the future. The few surviving and, unfortunately, diminishing ecosystem cultures have something to offer the rest of us: a view of life which fuses people and land into an indivisible whole in which our customs become extensions of our practice of living on home ground. As ceaseless growth invades Vermont, the victims are dairy farmers, one of the state's few commercial connections to homegrown food. Linny and I left Hartland and moved north to Blood Brook in part because Sally and Jack Comstock were forced by rising taxes and advancing age to subdivide their hillside farm and sell their old, sun-bleached house. Now, their son and daughter live in trailers on a shred of what was once Comstock acreage. In need of work, their grandchildren moved off the family homestead.

Twenty-five years ago, the upper end of Blood Brook drained

Marian and Floyd Godfrey's dairy farm. In the early 1970s, too old to farm, the Godfreys apportioned "Godfrey Heights" into five parcels. Eventually, Linny and I bought about seventy acres from several of the new absentee owners. Although troubled by the Comstocks' predicament, we had moved to second-growth woods that was once a farm, ambivalently pushing that same careening wheel that's everywhere turned against the land.

My goal, then, is to set deeper roots in Blood Brook Valley, to be more reliant on resources and products of my home region, while pruning some of my biosphere connections. And when I travel, to settle and step with the lightness of a red knot.

For thousands of years the Western Abenaki have lived in Ndakia, in the northeast corner of province 5. The names they give to the full moons—Sugar Making Moon, Berries Ripening Moon, Red Leaves Moon, Ice Forming Moon, Winter Coming Moon, for instance—evoke events that recur in the environs of Blood Brook as well as evoking images of a people whose myths encircle the planet.

The May 1991 issue of *Audubon* arrived in the mail recently containing editor Les Line's farewell address. After twenty-five years of introducing readers to "writing about natural history and conservation issues as *literature*, not merely information; to nature photography and painting as *art*, not merely pictures," Line's name is leaving the masthead of what is arguably the finest of the world's nature magazines. Having published some of the great "ecosystem" writers of the last quarter of a century—including Joseph Wood Krutch of the Sonoran Desert, John Hay of the Middle Atlantic Coast, Sigurd Olson of the western Great Lakes, Archie Carr of the southern bottomland forests, and Ann Zwinger of Rocky Mountain, Colorado—Line laments "that their work, even their names, are largely unknown by today's environmentalists and ecocrats, who would rather sort garbage than know the ways of a whooping crane, particularly if it meant actually *reading* a book or a magazine article."

The literature and art of nature and the myths of Indians are the wellsprings of environmental sanity, leading back into the earth itself. Intimacy with a piece of land, or a plant, or an animal can help correct counteract an attitude that lulls us into believing that we are apart from the seasons. For me, the earth begins at Blood Brook, but I must also reach across this valley, this watershed, beyond province 5, to wherever curiosity and fascination, both intellectual and material, lead me. Sorting garbage is necessary, is essential, but by itself will not, cannot, transform the environmental neonate into an ecosystem being.

When Ken Kesey was asked how he felt about NASA's space program, he replied that we don't deserve to be in space until we learn how to live on Earth. It will take concentration and several hours spent watching a red spider mite or a rose-breasted grosbeak—a bird that returned this morning to Blood Brook, having overwintered somewhere between south Louisiana and the Columbian Coastal Forest—to begin to show us how.

Acknowledgments

Many people have left their tracks on *Blood Brook* and the book is better for their efforts. Without Jim Schley's encouragement and editorial insights *Blood Brook* would have been different. Mark Humpal, John Hay, Ginny Barlow, Donna Nelson, Bruce Nelson, Tim Traver, Delia Clark, Hanford Monteith, Ginger Wallis, Bill Shear, Abbott Fenn, Steve Young, Rick Paradis, Joan Waltermire, and John Douglas gave me valuable advice on parts of the work-in-progess.

Portions of some of these essays first took form in *The Curious Naturalist*, published by the National Geographic Society; *Yankee*; *Harrowsmith Country Life*; *Vermont Magazine*; *Nature Conservancy*; *The Valley News*; and *Changing Hands, Changing Lands*, published by the Society for the Protection of New Hampshire Forests. These essays were enriched by suggestions from editors Tim Clark, Mel Allen, Tom Rawls, Wanda Shipman, Mark Cheater, Deborah Solomon, Anne Adams, Bruce Wood, Jim Fox, Nancy Serrell, and especially Jennifer Ackerman.

Petey Becker and David Laing answered my queries about glacial geology, William Brown about timber rattlesnakes, Bill Shear about spider webs, Susan Yost about ants and violets, Sandra Miller about fish, and Geoff Jones about hemlocks. Rick Shepp showed me Blood Brook from his glider. Michele Dionne showed me her damselflies and sunfish. Steve McAuslin loaned me videotapes of our trip to northern Quebec. Matthew Mukash introduced me to his people and their way of life. Mark DesMeules introduced me to timber rattlesnakes. Connie Rinaldo, head of the biomedical library collection service at Dartmouth College, engineered by computer literature searches.

I appreciate the work of the editorial team at Chelsea Green. Joni Praded commented on the first draft; Ian Baldwin and Helen Whybrow on every other one. Emily Wheeler copyedited the final draft, and Kate Mueller made copyediting suggestions. My principal editor, Jim Schley, suggested, challenged, and, in a few cases, insisted that *Blood Brook* address the nagging issues that keep me separate from my valley.

Patiently, Linny listened, read, and discussed the evolving book. Her comments and dedication to the project eased me through several emotional meltdowns. Thanks for the support.

So, Casey, I'm through. Let's play ball.

BLOOD BROOK
was designed and formatted in Goudy
by Kate Mueller/Electric Dragon Productions.
It was printed on acidfree, recycled paper by Maple-Vail.